# CONTENTS

D1594778

To Nicola and my children, who have
supported me all these years, and to Patrick Beaucé,
my co-founder in Objectile

# INTRODUCTION

# BY MARIO CARPO

In the late 80s and in the 90s of the last century, a handful of pioneers and visionaries began to think that a new generation of digital tools for design and manufacturing would change the history of architecture, and called for a new design theory. It now appears they were right. Bernard Cache was one of the first among them – both chronologically and in order of importance.

Of course, digital tools would have existed, and architects would have used them, even without the guidance of any related architectural theory. Indeed, many major architectural offices were already using sophisticated CAD systems even before Cache, and others, voiced any ideas on the matter. Historians may also argue that some embryonic theories on computer-aided design existed before the digital turn of the 1990s. But those theories that existed before the 1990s had little or no influence on design, and those offices that used digital tools did not use them to design anything new: they used them to design things that could equally have been designed without any computer at all. Many still do.

Today, in most countries around the world, scores of commonplace, banal and repetitive shopping malls and parking lots are designed and built using advanced BIM technologies. But few would see those buildings as inspirational examples of a new architecture for the digital age. Likewise, we could use digital technologies to rebuild an identical copy of the Seagram Building if we so chose, but that would not make any such replica a building of the digital age, either, as the original was manifestly built using

the notational and constructional techniques of the 1950s.
As a first approximation, new buildings of the digital age
are those that give the impression of having been built
using digital tools – or, more subtly, those that could not,
or would not, have been built without them. And in the
1990s the consensus among architects, and then also among
the general public, was that the use of digital technologies
in architecture almost inevitably led to, or involved, the
making of folds, blimps, bubbles and blobs. How did that
happen? Computers are versatile machines, and they can
make blobs as well as boxes. Why is it that at the beginning
of the digital turn and for some time thereafter (in some
cases, to this day) curvilinearity has been seen as the
hallmark of the digital in building?

   It would take the combined talents of a great
philosopher, a historian, a technologist and a designer
to try and account for the reasons of the pervasive and
resilient empathy between digital tools and the making
of curves. At the beginning, a classical philosopher, thinker
and polymath decided to study the history of calculus,
and a young architect with a background in mathematics
and economics decided to study philosophy with him.
When in 1988 Gilles Deleuze published his book on *The
Fold: Leibniz and the Baroque*, his former student Bernard
Cache was frequently cited in text and footnotes. To make
this long story short, Deleuze was apparently fascinated
by the notation of mathematical functions, particularly
parametric functions (which he also attributed, somewhat
generously, to Leibniz). From this fascination, and Cache's
feedback, arose two new ideas: the Objectile and the
Fold. Deleuze's (and Cache's) Objectile is a generic object:
an open-ended algorithm, and a generative, incomplete
notation, which becomes a specific object only when each
parameter is assigned a value. In the same way, a
parametric function notates a family of curves, but none
in particular. And as the functions Deleuze was dealing
with were continuous functions, their point of inflexion,
of Fold, is mathematically defined as the maximum or
the minimum in the first derivative of the function of the

curve (although Deleuze, curiously, did not define the point of inflexion in the abstract terms of modern differential calculus, but in visual and geometrical terms, as the point that separates concavity and convexity, or the point where the tangent intersects the curve).

The role of these notions in the grand scheme of Deleuze's thinking matters little here, as for most architect readers, who soon fell out of the picture (exceptions made for Deleuze's passing reference to the actual and often textile folds that characterised baroque painting, sculpture and architecture). More crucially for the history of design, however, Deleuze also cited Cache for noting that this mathematical definition of the Objectile corresponds to a very modern notion of the technical object: one attuned to the new digital tools for design and fabrication. And, due to the mathematics embedded in the first programs for CAD and animation that became widely available in the years that followed, anyone who started to tinker with them at the time would end up, almost inevitably, manipulating continuous functions, bending curves and splines through operations mostly reenacting the logic of calculus, and playing with points of inflexion – in the language of the time, Folds.

So here we have – as an integral part of an impervious book of philosophical hermeneutics dealing mostly with Leibniz's ontology and other metaphysical matters – an almost complete formulation of the conceptual bases that would drive digital design for the next 20 years: on the one hand, a procedural principle (the design of a generic, parametric notation); and on the other, a formal principle (the use of mathematics to script continuous functions, mostly represented by curving lines or surfaces). Another and equally quirky part of the story (which again, for brevity's sake, cannot be told here) is that this ground-breaking theoretical construction would have gone largely unheeded in the English-speaking world had it not been spotted and translated into more palatable architectural terms, and adapted to the deconstructivist thinking of the time, by Peter Eisenman, who would in turn pass it on to his gifted student Greg Lynn. Cache's own book, which Gilles Deleuze in 1988 had announced as forthcoming, was published only in 1995, and in English, as *Earth Moves*, the first volume in Cynthia Davidson's 'Writing Architecture' series, a project of the Anyone Corporation. Some of Cache's seminal writings of the 1990s were likewise published by the *ANY* magazine or in the ANY conference volumes.

This unlikely sequence of ideas and events, here too cursorily abridged, was the crucible where the digital turn in architecture took shape, and thence went on to become a major trend in global architectural design. Perhaps too global, as some of the very protagonists of this story would soon remark. Peter Eisenman has long forsaken – indeed, recanted – his early enthusiasm for most digital matters. And Bernard Cache, who was one of the masterminds at the origin of it all, effectively diverted a significant part of his subsequent work to fight against the drift, corruption and transmogrification of some of his early theories. This book bears witness to some of these efforts.

The first essay in this collection, 'Objectile: The Pursuit of Philosophy by Other Means?', written in 1999, epitomises the basics of the 'Deleuze connection' which upended architectural thinking in the 1990s. But in the second, 'Plea for Euclid', first published in 1998, Cache is already chafing at some of the most popular misconceptions of the digital vulgate of the time. When architects and architectural writers jumped on the 'cyberspace' bandwagon, William Gibson's sci-fi buzzword (of *Neuromancer* fame, 1984) gained new and sometimes unwarranted meanings. Cyberspace was then often seen as an alternative to actual architectural space – one where some physical laws of the latter, such as gravity, and congruency, did not apply. In retrospect, that seems to have been a dead end: even in fields where physical constraints could more easily have been neglected – in the development of video games, for example – designers have for the most part tried to simulate the bodily experience of space, or 'augment' it with additional layers of data – rather than invent disembodied alternatives. But in 1998 all that was still to come. Against the then popular seductions of cyberspace, Cache simply recalled that the architect's mandate, ultimately, is to design buildable things; and all things buildable, when built, must perforce inhabit a three-dimensional space which Euclid's geometry is still best at describing. As Cache then claimed, the geometrical transformations performed by digital tools are more complex than Euclid himself could have anticipated, but they are still fully accommodated by Euclidean geometry.

Having thus redefined the Euclidean ambit of a new digital tectonics, the fourth essay in this book, 'Towards a Non-Standard Mode of Production' (2003–05), returns to the troublesome issue of curvilinearity. Cache highlights here the generic (in the Aristotelian sense) and generative logic of the Objectile: parametric variations may eventuate in all sorts of series, regardless of their visual form – and certainly regardless of all opposition between angular and curvilinear. When CAD and CAM work in sync, digital technologies allow for the serial reproduction of non-identical parts, and mass-produced variations may come at no extra cost. Cache does not use the term 'mass-customisation', which predates the digital turn, and does not necessarily refer to digital non-standard seriality. He insists instead on the technical notion of associativity: using associative software, the design process is translated into a formalised generative system, where changes in a part can be automatically applied to the whole. This points to the vast discussion on parametricism that would follow, as in fact what today goes under the name of parametricism often derives from, or simply restates, Deleuze's and Cache's definitions of the Objectile. Cache also anticipates here the debate on data flow and collaboration that has become the staple of today's software for Building Information Modelling (BIM). Indeed, on many counts the logic of today's Building Information Modelling would curiously seem to satisfy Cache's own process-based agenda of the late 1990s and early 2000s. Developed in response to the actual managerial tasks of the building industry, BIM software extends the logic of non-standard production from small-scale fabrication and prototyping to the full scale of on-site construction and project delivery. Due to its very nature, BIM is also a notoriously bureaucratic tool, valued by cost-controllers but often scorned by designers.

As if in anticipation of, or response to, this shift to-wards performance and implementation, Cache adds here two essays, 'Geometries of Phàntasma' (2004–07) and 'Solidarity Without Proximity' (2004), where the exegesis of classical sources leads to a new take on his cherished theory of variations through geometric invariants. As else-where in the book, this derives from Felix Klein's general synthesis of geometry known as his Erlangen Programme (1872), which Cache abridges and reduces to four classes of geometrical transformations: isometric, proportional, projective and topogical. Ordered in a sequence, from the simpler to the more complex, these seem to evolve in time alongside the history of architecture itself, from classical isometry and proportionality to late-medieval stereotomy, from early modern perspective to contemporary digital topology. In one of his most vivid essays on this matter, not included here ('Digital Semper', 1999), Cache also relates these four ages of geometry, and of architectural history, to Gottfried Semper's taxonomy of the four elements and of the building materials and tectonic cultures deriving from them.

But in this teleology, the fourth stage (topology, which corresponds to the textile materials and to the technologies of weaving) occupies a specially ambiguous position, as the geometries of weaving are at the same time among the oldest and the newest: the first craftsmen in history (who in this instance were in fact craftswomen) knew how to weave and flex and bend textiles in convoluted and complex and rich forms that only the most advanced contemporary software can reenact (by mathematical notation and machinic fabrication). Once again, the pre-mechanical (craftsmanship and handmade variations) and the post-mechanical (computational making and digital variability) find themselves on an equal footing: the craftsman and the digital are friends, not foes. And in spite of Cache's proclaimed indifference to formal solutions, and equanimity towards the four geometries he itemises, one senses here the hints of an actual, if covert, aesthetic inclination. Topology is not simply one geometrical transformation among others – Cache seems at times to bestow upon the textile materials, and the cultural technologies derived from them, some metaphoric, poetic, almost redemptive virtue and valour. In 'Solidarity Without Proximity', for example, weaving and topological transformations even inspire strategies for contemporary urban governance and policy-making. Cache unearths this paradigm from sources at the very dawn of Greek classical history; but he also shows how, amplified in potency by today's digital tools, the logic of weaving could address some of the most pressing predicaments in today's cities, and societies.

Neither digital technologies, nor our societies at large, seem to be going in that direction. From their very beginning, in the early 1990s, digital technologies and their design applications have risen in sync with the neoliberal bend of most Western societies. This political development, which some used to call 'post-historical' (with regard to the evaporation of the socialist ideology in the aftermath of the fall of the Berlin Wall), and some still call 'post-industrial', or 'late capitalist' (but with different socio-technical implications), has been marked by growing differences in income between the haves and the have-nots in most Western societies; by the privatisation of services which in most countries used to be provided by states or communities – from education to health care, from pension plans to infrastructure (gas and water and electricity but also telephone, television and internet access); and by the deregulation of the production and marketing of most remaining goods and services (including, crucially, financial services).

In one of his latest essays, and the penultimate in this book ('Obama versus Irresponsibility'), Cache takes stock of some of these developments, measures their effect, looks for causes, and asks the crucial technological question – *post quem* or *propter quem*: is the digital turn casually or causally related to the neoliberal turn taken by most societies where digital technologies have taken root and thrived? One could easily assume that the chronological correlation between the rise of the digital and the rise of neoliberalism is accidental; hence, a different society or different political agendas could adopt the same technologies and put them to different tasks. But in the social history of technologies coincidences are seldom accidental. A new technology that no one needs or uses will not fly, and will go nowhere; in this sense, as anthropologist Leroi-Gourhan argued long ago, any invention is the making of a social group. When a new technological supply is successful, we must assume it matches some social or market demand, and if that is so, we must also conclude that for the last 20 years digital technologies must have served the neoliberal agenda well.

Even putting aside any such interpretive model, some more specific evidence of that causal connection would not be hard to find. Digital technologies allow for the mass-production of variations and promise endless customisation, at little or no cost, of all sorts of media objects and physical objects. But variations for whom? And what for? One could argue that in many cases where one size does not fit all, both literally and metaphorically, digital mass customisation fills a void and fulfils a real demand. Mass customisation (or, in Cache's terms, non-standard seriality) can save time, materials, energy and money; it can produce better and cheaper goods (including architecture) and services for more people, protect the environment, even save lives. Not a bad deal, one would say.

One could also argue that the trivial multiplication of unnecessary or unwarranted variations is wasteful, or worse: that it encourages egotism and individualism, weakens social bonds, fragments communities (or 'master narratives', or 'strong referentials') and may in the end 'decompose' the social fabric itself – or endlessly reshuffle its 'thousand plateaus'. Not coincidentally, this is also the very definition of post-modernity that François Lyotard, and to some extent Deleuze himself, set forth circa 1979–80.

Digital technologies also promised to implement an almost ideal, frictionless marketplace where demand and supply can always meet instantaneously, thus making market prices, and the 'invisible hand' of the market, more precise, predictive and trustworthy than ever before. This model need not be limited to financial transactions: Wikipedia and many other similarly constituted social or participatory media are based on the same persuasion, namely that a theoretically infinite number of unverified bits of information may result, through crowdsourcing, endless accumulation and digital mediation, in a superior body of knowledge. On the democratic wisdom of Wikipedia the jury is still out; but on the accuracy of the valuations provided by financial markets ante 2008 the verdict is already in.

So it appears that the financial bubble and the architectural blob may ultimately have more in common than mere batches of lines of computer code. Cache concludes his Obama essay with an act of faith and hopeful optimism: 'yes, we can' fight for a rational and responsible use of the new digital technologies; in design, digital technologies can be put to better uses than those they have been hitherto confined to. Yet this confident assertion is soon and somewhat perplexingly contradicted by the Vitruvius essay, the last in the book. Cache recently defended his French doctoral dissertation on Vitruvius' science and design method, and the resulting monumental typescript is now being readied for publication. A mere aside of that vast scholarly effort, this essay deals with Vitruvius' accounts of war machines and warfare in the last book of *De architectura* – and on the oddity of Vitruvius' tales on such matters no more will be said here, so as not to spoil the reader's discovery. Cache reveals a pattern of misrepresentation and possibly plain lying, which would not be the least of the many riddles that have made Vitruvius' treatise so impenetrable and baffling to modern readers, from Renaissance humanists to this day. Suffice it to say that Vitruvius suggests, at the very end of his book, that the rational logic of machines may have to be defeated by ruse, machinations and cheating; and that only sabotage may in the end help humans prevail against technology. Vitruvius stresses the point in his story of the siege of Marseille, where the citizens of one of the few remaining independent city-states in the Western Mediterranean fought for their freedom against Caesar's besieging army. In Vitruvius' tale, they won. In fact, they lost – and Caesar's war machines went on to extinguish Rome's own republican freedom, and to pave the way for five centuries of imperialism and tyranny. We all know the rest of the story.

Bernard Cache has been almost always right so far – history has already vindicated many of his sometimes precocious intuitions. Let's hope he is wrong this time around.

# PROJECTILES

What is the point of revisiting texts that are in some
instances already more than 10 years old? The short answer,
from the author's point of view, is that this compilation
provides a welcome opportunity to clarify our approach
– an approach that has had to be extremely flexible in light
of the rapid flux of contemporary geopolitics. The course
of this trajectory may not seem particularly clear from
day to day, but its coherence is reinforced by the multiple
cross-references between these texts, which were composed
in very different contexts. A brief consideration of the first
and last texts illustrates this point.

'Objectile: The Pursuit of Philosophy by Other
Means?' is a commemorative essay that aims to evoke the
extraordinary adventure of engaging with the thought of
Gilles Deleuze. It goes without saying that the mere
mention of this philosopher's name immediately provokes
huge misunderstandings, particularly when it surfaces in
the context of architectural theory. Anyone who ever visited
the two-storey apartment on rue de Bizerte where Deleuze
lived for many years will remember the tatty second-hand
chests of drawers, legs braced with electrical cable to
prevent them from collapsing. In the material spaces that
Deleuze inhabited there was nothing at all to suggest an
infatuation with a modernity of 'design' – though he did
play mischievously with the architecture of the apartment
so that you entered by one door and left by another. How,
then, has the name of Gilles Deleuze been able to serve
as a watchword for an apology for a technology-driven
architecture of spectacle that takes no account of the
historical and social layering of a city? That would be a
good subject of study for anyone interested in how ideas
become distorted. We have to admit that we have

contributed in a small way to this misunderstanding, since the introduction of computers into our discipline was like opening up a Pandora's box. Despite all our precautions – our insistence on the need to think through the means and relations of production; our attempt to tie these variable curved surfaces and sloping planes to historical precedents such as the baroque of a Leibniz or a Juan Caramuel y Lobkowitz – it has become all too clear that the digital in architecture is often reduced to a plaything for adolescents who dream of constructing a beautiful object, whatever the financial or social cost.

The most important thing enabled by the digital is not the design of beautiful curved surfaces, but rather the construction of a long chain of relations between the initial hypotheses of a project and its formal result – and this applies as much to an orthogonal architecture in the Hilberseimer mould as it does to 'curvy broken-style' architecture. It is therefore vital to objectify the concept of the project through a clear definition of hypotheses, relations and consequences. But it is futile to try to explain all this. For we're in a double-ended trap, sprung on the one hand by the Ancients and on the other by the modernists, especially the Italians. The rationalists of the 1970s and 1980s, who thought of architecture in terms of methods of production, were somehow unable to foresee that the most strategic component of fixed capital would not be the machines themselves but rather the software that drives them. As a consequence, the momentum of the architectural debate shifted to the United States, where the rapid rise of digital technology as an object of fascination was facilitated by the swing to hyper-liberalism and total imperialism. But it should be remembered that the information industry is not new – that a company like IBM is more than a century old, that its prewar director, in his capacity as president of the International Chamber of Commerce, opposed sanctions against Nazi Germany in 1937, proffering slogans such as 'only untrammelled commerce can assure world peace', and that during his tenure his company knowingly collaborated on the construction of the statistical category of 'Jew'.[1] Historical recollections of this sort are very badly received. There is practically no scope left for critical discourse in our globalised universities and cultural institutions: it is becoming harder all the time to find an outlet for a properly constructed argument based on a thorough examination of reasoning rather than mere sound-bites. The forces of media and politics have colluded to present as insignificant a death-toll of 300,000 in Iraq, in retaliation for the killing of 3,000 in New York. In the field of architecture, which prides itself on its globalisation, very few spoke out against a war that was not only completely immoral, but totally nonsensical from a military point of view – the US administration did not listen to the generals who had experience of the Vietnam conflict. More and more, rational discourse is submerged in a stream of soft propaganda from the media empires.

Curiously, this state of affairs leads us straight to the last text in this collection, 'Vitruvius, Machinator, Terminator'. For it is too often forgotten that the first theory of our discipline of architecture was the work of a military engineer who constructed war machines during a period when the Roman republic appeared to be giving way to the measured dictatorship of Augustus. Measured, because Augustus, having reflected on the reasons behind the assassination of his adoptive father Caesar, was careful not to appear to exceed his mandate. To deflect the suspicion that he was re-establishing a monarchy, he made sure that no powers were definitively attributed to him. Similarly, he knew how to make use of religion without being accused of seeking self-deification. Augustus also had a talent for surrounding himself with brilliant intellectuals – like Horace, or Virgil – who burnished the official ideological discourse of a return to the Golden Age. This was the context for the emergence of *De Architectura*, a first effort on the part of an architect to think of a project in rational terms, specifying the relations between all the components of a building or a machine – relations that, by definition, could only be proportional.

The first building mentioned in *De Architectura* is not a temple but the Tower of the Winds in Athens, which had a sundial on each of its eight faces, and an enormous anaphoric clock inside.[2] So, not only did Vitruvius devote his professional career to the construction of war machines, but the first structure that he presents is itself a machine, and not a machine for living in, but a machine for producing information. What interests us about this seminal treatise is that, far from being reducible to a theory of architectural orders, *De Architectura* gives us the possibility to construct a tradition based on the most innovative aspects of our discipline. For example, with Vitruvius' *ballistae*, the dimension of the hole through which the torsion spring was stretched was calculated as the cube root of the weight of the projectile – a calculation arrived at using machines such as Eratosthenes' mesolabe.[3] Thus we can see the roots of the digitisation of architecture in its very first treatise – a fact that should encourage a new reading of the history of our discipline.

However, the use of instruments to calculate modular relations in buildings that were thought of as machines did not prevent Vitruvius from maintaining a certain distance from all of this fine mechanisation. The same man who spent his waking hours constructing catapults and *ballistae* then finishes his treatise by recounting four sieges where the besieged had triumphed over their assailants and their formidable war machines.[4] The first western treatise on architecture therefore finishes with the spectacle, repeated four times, of machines foundering in inglorious mud – an anti-architecture of decomposition.[5] So it seems that we can find at the very heart of our written tradition the means both to construct a rational discourse and maintain a critical distance. We hope that the articles brought together here will illuminate how – inspired by our interest in developing the means of production for a non-standard architecture – we have been able to draw on antiquity to give our contemporary condition a historical depth that it seems otherwise to sorely lack.

NOTES

1. See Edwin Black, *IBM and the Holocaust* (Washington, DC: Dialog Press, 2009).
2. Vitruvius, *De Architectura*, I, 6, 4.
3. Vitruvius, *De Architectura*, IX, preface 14.
4. Vitruvius, *De Architectura*, X, 16, 12: 'Thus all these cities are liberated, not by machines, but by expedients which are suggested through the ready ingenuity of their architects. '*Ita eae uictoriae ciuitatum non machinis, sed contra machinarum rationem, architectorum sollertia sunt liberatae*'.
5. To describe this mud, Vitruvius twice uses the Latin word *stercus*: excrement, dung, manure.

# OBJECTILE: THE PURSUIT OF PHILOSOPHY BY OTHER MEANS?

Perhaps I'd best begin by unpacking the title of this essay. 'Objectile' was the name given by Gilles Deleuze to the research I am carrying out with Patrick Beaucé and others into the development of industrial means of producing non-standard objects.[1] By this, I mean objects that are repeatable variations on a theme, such as a family of curves declining the same mathematical model; objects in flux, inflected like the signal modulating a carrier wave; or lines and surfaces of variable curve, such as the folds of baroque sculpture or the decorative bands of plant motifs whose capacity for transformation was so convincingly demonstrated in Alois Riegl's history of ornament.[2] The 'pursuit of philosophy' refers to philosophy engaged as a mode of production – and not as a contemplative activity, and even less as an instrument of communication. 'Pursuit by other means?' The phrase consciously alludes to Carl von Clausewitz, reminding us not only that philosophy is a machine for waging war on any kind of apparatus, but also that our aims can easily be distorted by the means we use to achieve them – something that troubled the Prussian general (an avid reader of Kant). A neo-finalism as a philosophy of distortion – here, perhaps, is cause for celebration!

How is that philosophy subject to such distortion? There are probably many reasons, there seems to be no shortage of either causes or opportunities. Yet, like most, I detect one overriding factor: the computer. This is hardly a new denaturing force, however, for the seeds of the computer were not planted by Gaspard Marie Riche de Prony (1755–1839), who wanted to manufacture logarithms 'as easily as pins', or even by Charles Babbage (1791–1871), who found a way to mechanise the calculation of mathematical tables. Nor was it conceived during the Second World War – in the calculating rooms where the trajectories of ordnance were plotted – or even more latterly, in the garages of Silicon Valley. Rather, it took a philosopher like Leibniz to anticipate everything that contemporary computer science is only now beginning to realise. It was Leibniz who stated, clearly and brilliantly, that any form, no matter how complex, can be calculated. And it is this statement which validates our current attempts to design digitally – to conceive of 'objectiles' as declinations of parametric surfaces.

Philosophy as a calculation of reason and of forms, then. Having stated this goal, we now need to consider the means – systematic as well as material – required to achieve it. In terms of system, mention should be made of a largely forgotten giant of the history of science, Joseph Fourier (a contemporary of Charles Fourier), whose theorem made it possible to break up any periodic function into a series of trigonometric functions. It was Fourier who discovered the application for realising Leibniz's programme. All that remained was to implement the algorithms in high-performance silicon in order to automate the otherwise laborious calculation of series – FFT: Fast Fourier Transform. A French engineer, Didier LeGall, set up shop in the US, and his C-Cube Inc. developed the first digital compression circuits. The MPEG or H.261 video coding standards that underpin developments such as digital television and the videophone are nothing other than ultra-high-speed executions of Fourier transformations by integrated circuits. So one has to ask: how have these integrated circuits managed to distort a philosophical affirmation by processing a theorem in a fraction of a second behind our screens? This is just the kind of problem – related to the speed and the slowness of thought – that Gilles Deleuze loved to pose.

So let us rejoice in the face of this algorithmic Fourierism, for it signals, perhaps, that we have come to a turning point. We have to make the most of the fact that mathematics has effectively become a manufactured object, and when its components become photonic rather than electronic, the brakes will come off the speed of calculation. But the question is no longer simply one of the speed of calculation, which is potentially unlimited; what we now have to confront is the power or potency of calculation. Ought we to believe, then, the prophets of artificial intelligence who foresee a time when machines will think in our stead, and who claim that our consciousness is nothing but an epiphenomenon, more or less a parasite of algorithmic calculation? Is machinic thinking reducible to information processing? Are we on the threshold of a consciousness of a third kind, verging on that absolute or lightning speed of thought described by Gilles Deleuze in relation to the Fifth Book of Spinoza's *Ethics*? Or, are we heading instead towards a kind of explosion of thought where, having broken the calculation barrier, we soon discover a world in which algorithms no longer have any currency? In broaching these questions, one has to begin by saying that a computer does essentially two things: it calculates and it memorises. Calculation and Memory – not so different from Bergson's Matter and Memory. Let us examine each of these aspects in turn, starting with calculation.

Turing himself had already shown that there is a set of problems for which no algorithmic solution exists. As an example, we can cite a problem that is ostensibly very simple: 'Out of a set of polygons, which ones are suitable for tiling a plane?' This is a problem for a tiler or a mason, almost child's play: 'How do you cover a surface with a small number of basic shapes without leaving gaps or creating overlaps?' But it is also close to being a philosophical problem: 'How do you construct (a) space out of shapes rather than points?' Atomism posed the problem of constructing space on the basis of the point, understood as the means of reaching the limit of a shape so small that it has neither form nor parts. What daring! It is clear to us today that the problem is already very complicated when you start with divisible components, ie components with actual extension and form. Even if you restrict yourself to very simple elements – the juxtaposition of identical squares – there is no algorithmic solution to the problem of tiling a plane and worse still, a space, because of the occurrence of non-periodic elements. Such combinations of squares, known as polyominos,[3] will not form infinitely repeatable basic patterns, allowing one to tile a plane correctly. It was the British mathematician Roger Penrose who pointed out that the impossibility of solving tiling problems algorithmically was demonstrated by the fact that there was no general procedure for deciding when to 'switch off' a Turing machine. There are completely deterministic models of the universe, with well-defined rules of evolution, which are impossible to encompass algorithmically. Penrose then adds that the understanding of mathematics cannot be reduced to computation, and that comprehension is itself a non-algorithmic activity of the mind or brain. The most important consequence of Gödel's theorem is not the existence of unprovable propositions but rather the uncomputable element of thought, which can only be revealed in the most formalised domain, namely that of mathematical invention. Penrose builds on an argument advanced by John Searle: suppose that I manage to communicate, step by step, the basic elements of computer programming to someone who understands nothing about the field – partisans of artificial intelligence would claim that the computer 'understands' the algorithms it is processing, whereas it is clear that the user, even though he is the one who has written the program, persists in understanding nothing at all. This leads Penrose to propose the following:

> 1. Intelligence requires understanding.

> 2. Understanding requires an immediate knowledge of a different order from the writing of an algorithm.

In light of this, we might wonder whether the real achievement of the invention of computers has been to liberate thought from algorithms and the need to memorise things. André Leroi-Gourhan has talked about how the act of standing upright freed human jaws from prehensile and utilitarian functions, thus opening the way for the vocalisation of sounds to become the articulation of speech. In a similar fashion, *homo cyberneticus* seems well on the way to developing the strange new faculties of an amnesiac and analgorithmic consciousness. Gilles Deleuze was very much a philosopher of the twentieth century, in the sense that he knew how to ford this stream of mnemonic and algorithmic unconsciousness, picking his way from one stepping-stone to the next – from Bergson to Ruyer – finding in them confirmation of the value of a 'surveying' consciousness (*conscience de survol*).

What the twenty-first century may well reveal is that the strangest thing about thought is this *consciousness*. We may be about to perform a tremendous philosophical somersault that will lead to a revival of interest in consciousness – not in any role as the seat of Reason, but rather as the locus of an irreducible *unreasonableness*. Let us not forget that Enlightenment thinkers made Reason a conscious act, and equated a lack of Reason with a lack of conscious awareness, unbounded in law, but in reality limited. Then came the Romantics who intuited only too well the intrinsic limits of consciousness in face of an irrationality that would soon be relocated in the unconscious. Freud would attempt to salvage the situation by explaining that the unconscious is itself a second form of Reason, long before the structuralists came along to tell us that this unconscious is not only the reason for a troubled conscience, but is Reason itself: Engram with a capital E, and Algorithm with a capital A. Nevertheless, what annoyed Gilles Deleuze about psychoanalysis was not so much its take on the unconscious, as the absolute reign of the engram and of the algorithm – of the infantile memory and, later, of linguistic, anthropological and mathematical structuralisms. Say we accept that there is an irreducible unreasonableness at the heart of consciousness. What then? The next step is to oppose the ideology of Information with a philosophy of Incarnation. For an algorithm has first to be incarnated before it can be processed. Telecommunications engineers are well aware that source coding is only half the story. Any image, no matter how complex, can certainly be sampled and reduced to a highly compressed digital series thanks to Fourier transformations, but this digital series still has to be supported by a physical platform. The source coding has to be backed up by a channel coding. In fact any text, any sound, any image may in future be reduced to a digital series, but a bit-stream – a series of ones and zeros – is nothing until it is recomposed in a given platform, at a predetermined clock time. This is how a digital series can effectively become a sound on a stereophonic membrane or an image on a video screen; this is how the digital word is made analogue flesh. And this is how the new digital montages are created: no longer is a given sound coupled to a given image, as in the good old days of cinematography; instead, sounds are visualised or images heard in a chiasmus of perceptions.

For even the smallest perception is itself already composed of a multitude of vibrations. Bergson reminds us that the simple fact of seeing a colour or hearing a sound is already an act of memory which contracts a quantitative multitude into a qualitative multiplicity. But this is something entirely different from the engram-memory of our computers. The engram is nothing but a sequence of bits, whereas memory-contraction is the act by which we constitute our presence in the world by condensing a series of moments into the thickness of a duration. It is the act whereby a bit of information is incarnated through a perceptual support – retinal persistence, or after-images of our consciousness – and number becomes sound or image. However this process is impossible to understand unless one makes matter itself the object of the kind of distinction that is applied to memory. For matter is also dualistic. Bergson commended Berkeley's 'immaterialism': 'matter has no inside, no underside … it hides nothing, holds nothing … possesses neither power, nor virtuality of any kind … it extends as surface and coheres at every moment in everything it gives'.[4] Matter is thus simultaneously that by which everything is given, reducible to pure quantity, like Lucretius' black atoms, as well as that which constitutes the most relaxed membrane, the qualitative residue without which quantity does not exist. It is the minimal colour without which there is no black or white, the fundamental noise without which there is no signal.

The computer forces us to rethink the boundary not just between the two major Bergsonian concepts of matter and memory, but also between the two Leibnizian stages that Gilles Deleuze used to explain the fundamental difference between the pairings of virtual/actual and possible/real.[5] These two stages no longer separate monads from bodies, nor matter from memory; instead, they create a chiasmus which allows us to place algorithm and engram together, on the side of Information, while coupling membranes and temporal frequencies on the side of Incarnation. Thus you have on one side all that can be computed and written, and on the other elements which appear non-computable and non-samplable – to put it in negative terms – but which take on a positive aspect as Duration and Membrane. This works so well that we are tempted to propose a new version of the diagram sketched by Gilles Deleuze in *The Fold*, where he juxtaposes two very different processes: the actualisation of the virtual and the realisation of the possible. When it comes to the engram and the algorithm anything is possible – at least, so IT experts keep telling us. And possibilities press to become realities, subject only to rules of economic optimisation as calculated by the invisible hand of the market, which, as an added bonus, promises to select only the best of all possible worlds. However this overlooks the fact that there are algorithms that cannot be determined, and therefore propositions of which it is impossible to say whether they are contradictory or not, or, more exactly, whether they are compatible or not with another set of propositions. This is the irreducibly uncomputable. On the other hand, the possible cannot become real without becoming corporeal, without incarnating itself in a membrane and undergoing a change in its nature in accordance with the temporal stimulus driving it to realisation. 'That which cannot be divided without changing nature,'[6] is how Deleuze described this second process, whereby the possible cannot become real without something of the virtual becoming actual. This is why Duration has its own thickness, and the reality cannot be anticipated in the possibility.

Membranes and frequencies: these are the singular figures through which the virtual is actualised at the same time as the possible becomes real, without any guarantee that the best will be selected. Kandinsky used the term resonance to designate what is spiritual in art. He also clearly perceived the advent of information technology: 'As these means of expression [abstract forms] are developed further in the future… Mathematical expression will here become essential',[7] he announced in *Point and Line to Plane*. He also warned, 'There is, however, the danger that mathematical expression will lag behind emotional experience and limit it. Formulas are like glue, or like a "fly paper" to which the careless fall prey. A formula is also a leather arm-chair, which holds the occupant firmly in its warm embrace.'[8] Written in 1923, Kandinsky's remarks sound like a warning to those of us who spend our days in front of a computer screen.

To be sure, computation enables us to design forms as modulations of abstract surfaces whose frequency and membrane remain indeterminate for a time. After Kandinsky, we take Leibniz at his word when he says that all forms are computable. And the only means we need to achieve this are the ones prescribed by Fourier, that is, series of trigonometric functions. And when we want to design volumes, we use whole periodicities which cause surfaces to curl up on themselves. In this first stage, therefore, we make mathematical models that allow us to calculate the infinite permutations of the possible. In order to approach these 'worlds', whose functions are comprised as much of dimensions as of parameters, we have developed exploratory tools that generate series of video images corresponding to trajectories within these multi-dimensional universes. Objects generated by this process initially resemble still-frames from video footage.

But in order to move from these virtual possibilities to actual realities, we have to switch scanning techniques and replace the electronic remote control that activates the pixels on our video screen with a digital command router that manufactures any material. If we hear the term virtual reality so often, it is because video scanning appears to be the minimal machinic operation of the extremely ductile, supple membrane that is the video screen. We have to insist on the dual nature of this operation: first, it is already an incarnation, and secondly, the screen is just one membrane amongst many others. Hence video sequences are only a primary or first actualisation, which is why we can effectively speak of virtuality. The mathematical models that we are exploring still belong to the order of the possible and hold no surprises, except in the measure that our power of calculation remains limited. On the other hand, what we will never be able to predict is the relation between a frequency and a membrane. Selecting a still image requires us to assign a value to the parameters of our periodic functions in order to manufacture singularities in a series of objects in a specified material. Should the modulations on the surface of wooden panels be made larger or smaller in a given architectural context? Would a different modulation curl into a three-lobed volume in the middle of a room? How will the phase difference of an electron ripple relate to the texture of a predetermined membrane? Solutions to these problems cannot be anticipated, for in each case the actualisation differs in nature from all others, and in no case can the selection be optimised.

In a certain sense, none of this is really new. In fact, Mersenne's *Harmonie Universelle* of 1636 already asked whether one could compose the best song imaginable on the basis of an exploration of combinatorial principles. Mersenne concluded that it could not be done, because the number of possibilities was just too great – for example, the number of foreseeable melodies with 23 non-repeating notes already runs to the factorial of 23. Another example of combinatorics is the game of chess, where the number of permissible moves stands at 10 to the power of 56, a figure so large that it exceeds the number of electrons in the universe. The calculation of all of these moves thus remains unfeasible as long as computers are driven by electronic technology. If today's computers perform relatively well against flesh-and-blood opponents, it is because they use software programmed with heuristic devices that simulate a player's intuition on the basis of probabilistic hypotheses that limit the field of possibilities. But this does not count for much, since we can envisage that one day we will have quantum computers that will be unbeatable because they will be able to calculate all the possibilities. In essence, the problem of chess remains simple and eminently computable: it is a purely algorithmic problem based on a comparison of different possibilities with a view to selecting the best outcome – and thus purely a problem of realisation. Mersenne's musical problem is something quite different. We have long known that harmony is not defined once and for all, and that two notes which are considered consonant in the soprano range will be dissonant in the bass range, and that a chord which one composer finds dissonant will appear consonant to another. There is still no common basis for comparing musical modulations in the same way that we can weigh up chess moves. Leibniz proposed that the existence of a perfect major chord in one monad implies the existence of a minor or dissonant chord in another. But the procedure for selecting the 'optimum' solution out of all the different possibilities seems to be functioning less and less well. Thus, dissonance in one monad no longer implies consonance in another, to the benefit of universal harmony. On the one hand, the uncomputable element of algorithmic possibilities impedes selection by criteria of optimisation; on the other, the virtual cannot become real unless it undergoes a change in the nature of the membrane in which it is incarnated or the frequencies that animate it.

## PROJECTILES

As reality submits to ever more divergent actualisations, worlds jostle each other for space. And from this crush the notion of harmony is emerging as a singularity, rather than something universal. This is the basis of our attempt to put into practice a means of production for the non-standard.

### NOTES

1. The others being principally Jean-Louis Jammot, Charles Claeys and Christian Arber, all software developers at Missler Software.
2. Alois Riegl, *Problems of Style: Foundations for a History of Ornament*, trans. Evelyn Kain; annotations, glossary and introduction by David Castriota; preface by Henri Zerner (Princeton, NJ: Princeton University Press, 1993).
3. 'polyomino, n. The plane figure formed by joining unit squares along their edges. Polyominos all of which are congruent to a given polyomino that uses 4 or fewer squares can be used as tiles to cover a plane (ie monominos, dominos, trominos, tetrominos…)', from James and James (eds.) *Mathematics Dictionary* (New York, London: Chapman and Hall, 1992).
4. Gilles Deleuze, *Bergsonism*, trans. Hugh Tomlinson and Barbara Habberjam (New York: Zone Books, 1988), 41 (translation modified).
5. See especially *Bergsonism*, 42–43 and *The Fold: Leibniz and the Baroque* (London: Athlone Press, 1993), 105.
6. See *Bergsonism*, 40.
7. Wassily Kandinsky, 'Point and Line to Plane' in Kenneth C Lindsay and Peter Vergo (eds.), *Kandinsky, Complete Writings on Art, volume II* (1922–1943), (Boston, MA: GK Hall, 1982), 544.
8. Ibid.

# PLEA FOR EUCLID

Of course, we cannot be sure that space exists as such, nor can we affirm anything of its substance. Some would even deny that things exist; for them, perceptions are just mental events. Nevertheless, we know that there are differences in our perception. A diversity of things are thought before we even think of ourselves as the subject of that thinking. The Leibnizian *cogitata* comes prior to the Cartesian *cogito*. And, following Kant, space is the form according to which we organise variations in what occurs to us simultaneously, just as time is the form according to which we organise variations in what occurs in succession. Kant thought that Euclidean geometry was the ultimate organisation of this form of intuition we call space. But some 20 years after Kant died in 1804, several mathematicians working independently – Gauss, Bolyai and Lobachevsky, among others – discovered that we can think of other geometries. These non-Euclidean geometries were based on counter-intuitive assumptions and at first were thought of as nothing but mathematicians' games. But less than 100 years later, Einstein found that in his theory of general relativity, space was better described by using a complex variant of Lobachevsky's geometry. And as this theory of relativity was given very precise experimental validation, non-Euclidean geometry proved its relevance and could no longer be dismissed as an exotic logic.

What are the consequences of this evolution of mathematics for architects? Do we have to banish the five Euclidean postulates as an outdated heritage from the Greeks, just as the moderns dismissed the five orders of architecture? (The moderns made allusion to other geometries, but with very few tangible results.) And nowadays, in our digital age, does the computer compel us to think and live in a multidimensional, non-Euclidean, topological space? Or should we instead consider the computer as a variable compass that will open up new potentialities within the old Euclidean space? These questions require that we investigate in close detail what happened to geometry, and the answers are all the more important in as much as geometry still remains the very basic tool of architecture.

Euclid wrote the 13 books of his *Elements of Geometry* some 300 years before Vitruvius composed his own *Ten Books of Architecture*. This certainly makes Euclidean geometry one of the oldest works of science. Moreover Euclid did not start from scratch. Many of the theorems he uses were known long before his time, by the Egyptians in particular, whom the Greeks always held in great respect. What Euclid did, what was profoundly original, was to systematise a corpus of formerly isolated theoretical demonstrations and practical solutions. In fact, Euclid's work has two faces: on the one hand, it is a description of space both as a form of intuition and a physical phenomenon; on the other, it constitutes one of the first major works of logic. Hence the double evaluation required by the *Elements of Geometry*, both axiomatic container and physical content. As such, the *Elements* are a first attempt to link together abstract logic and sensual experience, bearing witness to the multiple origins of geometry, as Michel Serres reminds us.[1]

I will begin with the physical face of geometry. The dismissal of Euclidean geometry by architects seems rather surprising when one notices how much it is appreciated by contemporary scientists, even those who cannot be suspected of orthodoxy, such as Roger Penrose. In his book, *The Emperor's New Mind: Concerning Computers, Minds and the Laws of Physics*, Penrose argues that Euclidean geometry comes first in the list of the very few theories which deserve the label 'superb' for their phenomenal accuracy. Einstein's theory certainly teaches us that space(–time) is actually 'curved' (ie not Euclidean) in the presence of a gravitational field, but generally, one perceives this curvature only in the case of bodies moving at speeds close to that of light. Hence the very limited impact of Einstein's theory on technology. Normally, 'over a metre's range, deviations from Euclidean flatness are tiny indeed, errors in treating the geometry as Euclidean amounting to less than the diameter of an atom of hydrogen!' As those familiar with the difficulties created at a building site by the 1/10 millimetre accuracy of numerically controlled components surely know, Euclidean geometry is a more than sufficient approximation of architectural space. Our experience is that free curvature surfaces in architecture require rigorous accuracy, but we still have a way to go before trespassing the boundaries of Euclid's description. Lobachevsky himself undertook to submit geometry to experimental verification. Having plainly assumed the consequences of non-Euclidean geometry, he was conscious that geometry was a matter of choice, where intuition had nothing to dictate to logic. Nevertheless, with the physics and experimental accuracy of his time, Lobachevsky concluded that Euclidean geometry was the best model of space. By which we see that our trivial intuition is rather well suited to what we experimentally build up as a reality of space. As Einstein put it, 'What is incomprehensible is that the world is comprehensible.'

Now, when it comes to the other aspect of the *Elements*, following the *more logico* rather than the *more geometrico,* things become a bit more complex. Euclid started his work with 'definitions', 'postulates' and 'common notions', which form the basis of all of his theorems or propositions. The 23 definitions introduce terms that range from the 'point' as 'that which has no part' to the 'parallel' as 'coplanar straight lines which never meet'. These five postulates are:

To draw a straight line from any point to any point.

To produce a finite straight line continuously in a straight line.

To describe a circle with any centre and distance.

That all right angles are equal to one another.

That, if a straight line falling on two straight lines makes the interior angles on the same side less than two right angles, the two straight lines, if produced indefinitely, meet on that side on which the angles are less than two right angles.

Some common notions of arithmetic and logic are then introduced, such as:

Things which are equal to the same thing are also equal to one another.

The whole is greater than the part.

In fact, definitions, postulates and common notions each create their own problems. We will analyse these chronologically, as they have been confronted in the history of mathematics, ie, starting with the postulates.

From the beginning, readers of Euclid have been puzzled by the fact that he seems to shun his own fifth postulate, since he makes no use of it in the first 28 propositions. The first four postulates make it possible to construct figures and conduct demonstrations with a compass and ruler; these were easily accepted.[2] The belated use of the fifth postulate led commentators to think that it was not really necessary, that one could either get rid of it, or prove that it was a consequence of the first four postulates. Proclus (fifth century CE) already mentioned Ptolemy's attempt at emendation (second century CE), and proposed his own method. But for more than two thousand years all attempts proved unsuccessful until an Italian Jesuit priest, Girolamo Saccheri, published a little book titled *Euclides ab omni naevo vindicatus* (Euclid Freed of Every Flaw) in 1733. Saccheri used his earlier work in logic to undertake a *reductio ad absurdum*, trying to demonstrate that the negation of this unfortunate postulate would lead to contradiction. In so doing, not only did Saccheri not find any logical contradiction, but he actually demonstrated many theorems of what we now know as non-Euclidean geometry. However, the geometrical consequences of what he established were so unexpected and so contrary to general intuition that he concluded that he had discovered propositions 'at odds with the nature of the straight line'. Saccheri was so anxious to vindicate Euclid that he took these unexpected geometrical results for the logical contradiction he was looking for.

By 1763, Klugel was able to list – and criticise – up to 28 different attempts to solve the fifth postulate problem. The main result of these investigations had been to produce equivalent forms of the fifth postulate, the most promising being that of Playfair, a Scottish physicist and mathematician (1748–1819), who reformulated it as the Parallel Postulate: 'Through a given point P there is a unique line parallel to a given line.' It was under this new form that several mathematicians, working independently at about the same time, would resolve the problem of the fifth postulate. Gauss, Lobachevsky and Bolyai each demonstrated that no logical contradiction would arise with the other four postulates, no matter how many parallels to a given line pass through a given point. Spatial intuition would have to adapt to each case. The four postulates constitute what is called the 'absolute geometry' after which geometry bifurcates. Once this absolute geometry is assumed, you can stay within Euclidean geometry and assume that the number of parallels is only one; or you can state that there are no parallels, which leads to the 'elliptic geometry' of Riemann; or you can postulate that there is more than one parallel, which opens the doors to Lobachevsky's 'hyperbolic geometry'.

The paradoxical effect of non-Euclidean geometries was that they served to consolidate Euclid's authority. It was certainly no longer the only geometry, but they had proved that the fifth postulate was not only necessary but essential in making the logic of Euclid coincide with general intuition. For other geometries, the problem would be the opposite, ie to find intuitive models that would suit their logic. To do so, one had to jettison the usual signification of terms like point, line or plane. For instance, in Poincaré's model of hyperbolic geometry, lines become arcs of a circle, and in the spherical model of elliptic geometry, points are pairs of diametrically opposed points. Far from providing intuitive support to the logical demonstrations of non-Euclidean geometries, primary terms like points or lines are deduced from the system in which they are used. Primary terms are indefinable, just as postulates are undemonstrable. Hence the necessity of tracking every remaining spatial intuition in the *Elements* of Euclid.

This will be the great achievement of Hilbert in his *Grundlagen der Geometrie*, published in 1899: geometry becomes axiomatic. Hilbert based his system on 21 axioms which he organised into five groups, the number five establishing a continuity with Euclid's work. The first group, *projective geometry*, is composed of eight axioms which establish the *relations* between, rather than the *definitions* of, the concepts of points, lines and planes. For instance, one will find that the proposition, 'Two distinct points determine a unique line', can be converted in the converse relation, 'Two distinct lines determine a unique point'. This principle of duality was developed by Poncelet, who systematised the projective geometry of Desargues. The second group, *topology*, gathers the four axioms of 'order' establishing the meaning of 'between'. If $A$, $B$ and $C$ belong to the same line and $B$ is between $A$ and $C$, then $C$ is also said to be between $C$ and $A$. The third group, *congruence*, gathers the six axioms needed to define geometrical equality. The fourth group holds one unique axiom, which is the famous parallel postulate. And finally, the last group is made up of the two axioms of continuity, including Archimedes' axiom.

Combinations of these 21 independent and consistent axioms enable one to generate many geometries. Euclidean geometry is based on the totality of the 21 axioms and it has been proved that this logical system is saturated, which means that you cannot add a twenty-second axiom without creating contradictions in the system. Non-Euclidean geometries can be generated either by the negation or the suppression of one or several of these 21 axioms, for example by the negation of the uniqueness of the parallel postulated in the fourth group. One can also investigate non-Archimedean geometry by negating Archimedes' axiom in the fifth group. When it comes to suppressing axioms, we get a more general but also less structured geometry. Felix Klein showed that projective geometry is independent of the Parallel Postulate, which means that there can be both a Euclidean and a non-Euclidean projective geometry. Topology, in turn, is based on an even more restricted number of axioms. This is easier to understand when we look at geometry from another angle.

At about the same time that non-Euclidean geometry was discovered, Evariste Galois (1811–1832) established the theory of groups that Klein later applies to geometrical transformations. Klein goes so far as to define the various geometries based on the group of transformations which leaves invariant certain properties of geometrical figures. For instance, translation, rotation and symmetry form a first group of transformation, the group of movements which transform geometrical figures without affecting distances nor angles in these figures. This group of movements defines what is called 'metric geometry'. Now, if we forget the distances and concentrate on the 'shapes' of the figures defined by the angles between elements, we come upon a new transformation, which is the scaling. Translation, rotation, symmetry and scaling form a wider group of transformations, the group of similitudes that defines Euclidean geometry. Continuing in this fashion, there is a third group of transformations that assimilates the circle, the ellipse, the parabola and the hyperbola as sections through a cone. This corresponds to the common notion of perspective that a circle should be drawn as an ellipse when seen obliquely: deciding whether our eye is able to recognise circles perceived on the slant has been an important debate in architecture.[3] Juan Caramuel de

Lobkowitz went so far as to propose columns of oval section in order to correct for perspective effects in his counter-proposal for the colonnade of St Peter's in Rome. Getting rid of distances and angles, and focusing on what are called 'position properties' as opposed to 'metric properties', allows us to add projections and sections to the group of similitudes. This results in the group of homologies that defines projective geometry. And finally, if we do away with position, and only look at the continuity of figures and at the order in which their elements are linked – just as if figures were made of an elastic material that can be stretched and deformed, but not torn – we encounter another group of transformations: the homeographies that define topology.

In Klein's theory of transformation, as in Hilbert's axiomatic, there is a hierarchy among the various geometries. Between Euclidean and non-Euclidean geometries (of Riemann and Lobachevsky), there is only a question of specifying the form of the Parallel Postulate: it is a separation between equivalent geometries of the same level. Among Euclidean geometry, projective geometry and topology, on the other hand, there is a relation of inclusion in terms of both number of axioms and relevant geometrical properties left invariant by a certain group of transformations. Euclidean geometry requires more axioms and more structured properties; projective geometry and topology can be more general only to the extent that they deal with looser transformations and objects. As such, topology enables one to focus on fundamental properties from which our Euclidean intuition is distracted by the metric appearances. Because topology does not distinguish between a cube and a sphere, it focuses on what is left – order and continuity – and makes obvious the difference between the sphere and the torus. Of course, order and continuity are also essential to Euclidean geometry. Euclidean geometry includes topology, which is less than Euclidean geometry. Common misperceptions of the two result from the fact that topology focuses on properties which typically lead to complex, interlaced figures or, we could say, figures that appear all the more difficult to draw since perspective is no longer taught to the general public. Let us take an example which should appeal to architects. The Moebius strip has now become common-place in contemporary architecture, although in most projects it remains more a rhetorical figure than a geometrical structure. But there is one well-known building with a rather complex topological structure that has been overlooked: the Beaubourg in Paris. This scaffolding-building is certainly not original by virtue of its machinic image, which is simply a revival of the utopian drawings of Archigram. Nor does it fully function as an urban machine, since no advantage has been taken of possible connections with the underground passing alongside the eastern facade. However, using this building induces a very specific experience for anyone who ventures higher than the ground floor. In this case, you would enter by the main entrance – provided you know where it is – and, in so doing, you would not pass directly inside but would remain in a kind of exterior space that is already in the interior of the building. This mixed situation arises from a series of conditions, such as the vastness of hall, the stains of rainwater on the grey carpet, or the streams of people in coats heading chaotically to the escalators where, strangely enough, the inverse situation arises. The escalators obviously take people back to the outside, suspending them in the air while they contemplate the skyline of Paris and again confronting them with the weather, but even so, these escalators are more inside than the main hall is. The narrow dimensions of the tube, its circular section, and the stillness of the people standing on the mechanical steps while starting to take off their coats, all help to create an atmosphere that is cosy, sometimes to the point of being oppressive. It is only when one enters the rooms of the museum or of the library that one really feels inside, freed from this tension between interior and exterior. To recapitulate: one comes from the outside and enters an external interior before finally getting inside. This spatial experience has the topological structure of a Klein bottle. To what extent this topology has been taken into account in this particular architecture is another question, but the fact is that this structure can actually be built in Euclidean space. Moreover, this Klein bottle can take many shapes. One single topological structure has an infinity of Euclidean incarnations, the variations of which are not relevant to topology, and about which topology has nothing to say. New topological structures can be incarnated in Euclidean space as squared figures as well as curved figures. Topology cannot be said to be curved because it precedes our ability to assign metric curvature. Because topological structures are often represented with indefinite, curved surfaces, one might think that topology brings free curvature to architecture, but this is a misunderstanding. When mathematicians draw those kind of free surfaces, they mean to indicate that they do not care about the actual shape in which topology can be incarnated. This should open the minds of architects and allow them to think of spatial structures before styling them as either curved or squared. And of course as soon as it comes to actually making a geometrical figure out of a topological structure, we enter into Euclidean geometry: that is, the design of complex curvature is essentially Euclidean. One should not think of Euclidean geometry in terms of cubes as opposed to the free interlacing of topology. On the contrary, it is only when variable curvature is involved that we start getting the real flavour of Euclid, that suddenly the trivial concept of the unique parallel starts playing tricks on you. Willingly or not, architects measure things, and this implies a metric. To be sure, we may want to remind ourselves of the formless topological background common to all saturated geometries, Euclidean or otherwise. But this reminder demands accurate work on curvature. Only by mastering the metrics can we make people forget Euclid.

Let's now take another example at the scale of the territory. Paul Virilio has rightly emphasised the importance of speed in the perception of territory. Hence the interest in isochrone maps, which deform territories such that Bordeaux, for instance, appears much closer to

Paris than Clermont-Ferrand because it benefits from a high-speed rail link. These isochrone maps certainly give shape to the perception of geographical space by train travellers. We could go even further and use a 3D curvature to manifest the coexistence of fast tracks with slower means of communication. We would then get a kind of Riemann surface with a tunnel directly linking Paris to Bordeaux, while the slower means of communication would be inscribed on the outer distended surface of the tunnel. All these phenomena are certainly topological, since it is a question of modified distances that have an impact on order and continuity. Moreover, the maps are a spatial representation of distances measured in time. This is very different from the Beaubourg example, where we proposed a spatial structure for an architectural space. And indeed, topology can be very useful in analysing phenomena which are not restricted to the three dimensions of space. But note that the folded surfaces and tunnels of isochrone maps can easily be represented in 3D Euclidean space – the maps simply substitute a new mode of representation for the more traditional one. It is a sign of the richness of Euclidean space that it can accommodate various representations.

In terms of understanding multidimensional phenom-ena, and gaining a ready intuition of them, 3D Euclidean space remains the best geometric vehicle. Not that we want to repeat Kant's error of saying that Euclidean space is the unique form of spatial intuition; we cannot avoid the fact that there is a highly positive feedback between our Euclidean intuition and the experimental behaviour of physical space. We should keep in mind mathematicians' satisfaction when Poincaré provided a Euclidean model of Lobachevsky's geometry. In his dialogue with Bertrand Russell, Poincaré (who certainly cannot be suspected of empiricism) would conclude that 'Euclidean geometry is not true but is the fittest',[4] and this for two reasons: first, it is objectively the simplest – just like a polynome of the first order is simpler than a polynome of the second order – and then it suits the behaviour of solid bodies and light rather well. Poincaré would even go so far as to justify the limitation of our experience to three dimensions by relating it to the combination of the two-dimensional surface of our retina with the single independent variable of our muscular efforts to focus on objects according to their distance. In a world where the accommodation and convergence of our eyes would require two different efforts, one would certainly experience a fourth dimension in its visual space. It is perplexing, then, to hear of non-Euclidean interfaces in cyberspace. One is struck by the pregnancy of very traditional spatial metaphors like the double-pitched house or the village – interfaces much more 'heimat' than 'cyber' – in telecommunication laboratories working on interfaces with so-called virtual space. But Euclidean space has nothing to do with these traditional spatial archetypes. We believe – and have confirmed through our work in computer-aided design and manufacturing – that we won't invent new architectural space without going deeper into Euclidean geometry. Sure, we can think of multidimensional topologies which exceed the capacity of 3D Euclidean space, but multidimensionality is not the exclusive privilege of topology: there are Euclidean hyperspaces just as there are projective hyperspaces. But as far as architectural practice is concerned, we think about the way in which we use, translate or plunge multidimensional spaces of all kinds into 3D new Euclidean figures. Objectile, for example, uses everyday mathematical functions with a great number of parameters in order to design 3D surfaces. The aim of our work is not to create 'multidimensional, topological, non-Euclidean virtual spaces' but to design interfaces between parametric hyperspaces and incarnated 3D Euclidean figures.

Analytical tri-dimensionality is not outdated, even in Euclidean geometry. The principle of locating a point on a plane with two coordinates was already known to the Greeks, but the real use of coordinates required that a relationship be established between those two numbers. Nicolas Oresme, Bishop of Lisieux, who died in 1382, was probably the first to really introduce rectangular coordinates (which he called longitude and latitude) and to establish relations like the equation of the straight line.[5] He went further, extending his system of coordinates to 3D space and even to a kind of four-dimensional space, but he lacked the analytical formalism of Descartes (1596–1650) and Fermat (1601–1663). The bi-univocal correspondence between points in the Euclidean space and three-number sets $(x, y, z)$ would later be called Cartesian space, although real analytical geometry would only show up in the eighteenth century. It was only in 1700 that the equation for a sphere was first written. Up to then, analytical geometry had been limited to the plane and ignored 3D space. Descartes kept on mixing the analytical procedures and geometrical methods that he used for elements of the first order (straight lines and planes). Leonard Euler's *Introductio in analysis infinitorum* (1748) was the first work to establish the principle of equivalence of the double axis, $x$ and $y$; before that, the abscissa had been privileged over the ordinate. And it was not until 1770 that Lagrange wrote the equations for a straight line and plane in a system with three equivalent coordinates. Fully isotropic 3D space is, then, only 240 years old, originating somewhere between Claude Perrault's *Ordonnance des cinq espèces de colonnes selon la Méthode des Anciens* (1683), which made the architectural orders a convention, and Durand's *Précis des leçons d'architecture* (1802–05), which based architectural composition on an open system of axes. The grid is an ancient and fundamental element which can be found in the *castrum romanum* as well as in the vertical column and the horizontal entablature (not to mention the striking formal analogy between the Christian cross and the Cartesian system of the $x$–$y$ axis). But it took a very long time for this formal element to assume its current status of abstract grid, and we suspect it will be some time before all of the consequences of this *cartesianisation* of Euclidean space are understood.

The same slow-moving history happens with projective geometry, which is only just starting to be integrated into CAD software. At about the same time that Descartes initiated analytical geometry, a French architect,

Sieur Girard Desargues de Lyon, had the idea to transpose the methods of perspective in geometry. Two hundred years later Poncelet, an officer in Napoleon's army, used his captivity in Russia to undertake a synthesis of projective geometry. In his *Brouillon* ('Rough Draft') project of 1639, Desargues made a unified system out of the four conical curves. To be sure, the circle, the ellipse, the parabola and the hyperbola had been known since antiquity. The Greek Apollonius thought of them as sections of a cone, the basis of which was a circle. Nevertheless, these curves were studied separately, each thought to constitute a specific case, with prime importance assigned to the circle, as the perfect figure. Likewise, in architecture, Borromini would still use the arcs of a circle to compose the ovals of San Carlino alle Quattro Fontane instead of drawing real ellipses, which had been reintroduced into the Renaissance by Baldasarre Peruzzi.[6] In 1604 Kepler had been the first to use the concept of a point at infinity, which enabled him to describe the closed, finite figures of the circle and ellipse as well as the open, infinite parabola and hyperbola. But Kepler still thought of geometry as a symbolic system, and the continuum that linked the conic sections was still oriented towards the perfection of the circle. Only Desargues would dispense with the symbolism of the figure and reveal the consequences of the point at infinity. The circle became just one particular case of the various conicals which could be transformed into any other conical by projections and sections. Parallels would now intersect like any other line and converge towards a point that was now understood to be just like any other point on the plane. This secularisation of infinity was not particularly welcome. Desargues would encounter considerable opposition from artists, metaphysicians and mathematicians, with a few notable exceptions like Pascal and Mersenne. The Académie de Peinture, led by Le Brun, would oppose the approach to perspective in which things are drawn according to geometrical rules rather than empirical perception. Hence the reluctance to accept that a circle seen from an oblique angle transform into an elliptical figure with its own consistency. Hence the emphasis on the optics of the *perspectiva naturalis*, where the remoteness of objects is rendered by fading colours rather than by the rigorous geometrical constructions of the *perspectiva artificialis*. The metaphysicians, for their part, could not accept the assimilation of the infinite – considered a divine attribute – to common points of the plane. Guarino Guarini, architect and abbot of the counter-reformation Theatines order, invented methods to draw complex figures with only finite points. And even mathematicians like Descartes would show some reluctance to think of parallels as converging lines. Taken up by only a few disciples like La Hire, the work of Desargues would fall into oblivion, and it was not until the end of the eighteenth century that projective geometry would meet with renewed interest from Monge, Carnot, Chasles and especially Poncelet and von Staudt.

Poncelet would develop in space what Desargues had demonstrated in plane. He enunciated the fundamental principle of duality by asserting that every theorem involving points and planes has a shadow theorem that can be deduced by swapping the words *point* and *plane*. Later, the principle of duality would assume its most general form with the nine axioms put together as the postulates of projective geometry by Hilbert. Swapping *points* and *planes* enables us to replace the three first axioms by the next three. The swap does not alter the remaining postulates. Stepping back from axiomatics, we can say that projective geometry studies the effect of the two types of homographic transformations (projections and sections) on the variety of Euclidean space to which have been added points at infinity. Poncelet would use these projections and sections to develop theorems already demonstrated for simple figures like circles, and extend them to all conicals or curves of the second order. This general method of considering curves of order $n$ would pave the way for spaces of curves. For instance, points, circles and straight lines form a four-dimensional space in which they are assimilated to circles of zero, finite and infinite radius, which allows one to manipulate these three elements with the same mathematical methods. And based on the principle of continuity, Poncelet would further assume that theorems established for finite and real figures also apply to infinite and imaginary cases. Thus the extension of Euclidean space to infinite points is complemented by another extension to imaginary points. In this way, for example, the radical axis defined by the points of intersection between two circles can continue to exist as an imaginary axis even when the circles no longer overlap.

Poncelet was very attached to spatial intuition and wanted to develop projective geometry as an autonomous discipline, independent of algebraic analysis. But the evolution of mathematics did not cooperate. Projective geometry benefited from the same algebraic methods that applied to Euclidean space in Cartesian geometry. All points of projective space would associate to four numbers, $X$, $Y$, $Z$, $U$, the fourth one enabling the addition of points at infinity to Cartesian space; those numbers would be either real or imaginary to take into account imaginary solutions in equations of intersections. Projective geometry would then become an algebra that was developed for its own sake, mathematicians forgetting the spatial significance of their investigations. Meanwhile, CAD softwares appeared in the 1960s and their structure remained strictly Cartesian. Suffice it to say that the twin brother of CATIA is EUCLID.[7] As far as technical applications such as architecture are concerned, the digital age is still deeply Euclidean and will probably remain so for all the reasons we have rehearsed. For instance, as CAD software becomes parametric and variational, designers can start to implement topological deformation into Euclidean metrics, which means that you can now stretch a model and still maintain control of its metric relations. What will probably happen is that, one day or another, CAD software kernels will benefit from the extension of Euclidean space within projective geometry. A Canadian company has already started developing the most advanced CAD software kernel on the basis of these ideas. Not by chance is this company called SGDL, which stands for Sieur Girard Desargues de Lyon: since this team of software developers spends time reading centuries-old writings on mathematics. They have already developed a single interface that enables the manipulation of points at infinity and thus unifies the various primitives, each of which is the object of a dedicated function in traditional software. The great primary forms that constituted Le Corbusier's Roman lesson in *Vers une architecture* – the cylinder, the pyramid, the cube, the parallelepiped and the sphere – together with more sophisticated figures like the torus, are no longer isolated archetypes but can be seen as particular cases in the continuum of the quadrics. More generally, one can notice in the field of mathematics a strong return to geometry initiated by eminent figures like Coxeter, so much so that future CAD software, rather than becoming non-Euclidean, will benefit from all the extensions of Euclidean space into Arguesian geometry. As such they will integrate the concepts we have mentioned above: points at infinity, imaginary points and multidimensional spaces of curves and surfaces.[8]

One last parenthesis about the fundamentals of geometry before considering how the digital age could show us the real flavour of Euclidean space rather than dissolve it. While examining how Euclid's 13 books have been reworked throughout the history of mathematics, we first looked at the postulates and their axiomisation by Hilbert. This led us to the fact that the primary terms of geometry should no longer be subject to definition because their signification would just be a consequence of the relations established by the axioms. But, up to now, we haven't said a word about the common notions by which Euclid referred to arithmetic and logic. Hilbert's axiomatic geometry also relies on basic notions of arithmetic and logics. There is a hierarchy of axiomatic systems by which geometry includes an arithmetic, which in turn includes a logics. As a direct consequence, geometry suffers from the same flaws as its presupposed axiomatics. Thus geometry is spoilt by the same incompleteness that Gödel demonstrated for arithmetic: there are true propositions that cannot be proved as such, and remain undecidable within the system itself. But Gödel demonstrated that this is a general flaw of all powerful axiomatics, which doesn't specifically affect Euclidean geometry. For instance, arithmetic suffers from the same flaw and, to our knowledge, very few people take advantage of this incompleteness by making claims for a non-Peanean arithmetic. Moreover, in 1937 Gentzen reestablished the coherence of the theory of numbers by using one single principle referring to an intuition exterior to the formal system. Incompleteness can be cured by a limited recourse to intuition. We have seen to what extent modern physics has validated Euclidean intuition, and we now realise that even its logical structure should not be called into question anymore than logic itself. However we approach it, Euclid's *Elements*, after more than 2,000 years, still appears to be the best available theoretical and practical tool for dealing with figures in space.

From this perspective, then, is the contemporary rejection of Euclid merely an academic matter, just another strategy of the avant-garde? Is it a *tabula rasa* of space that seeks to succeed the *tabula rasa* of time through which the Moderns sought to rid us of the past? We have seen how the controversy about projective geometry in the baroque era was already architecture and still philosophy. All the same, we can suspect that when a proposition as errant as non-Euclidean architectural space becomes so widespread, it bears the value of a symptom. The truth of this symptom seems to indicate that we have lost the will or, at least, the strength and the ability to establish distance, not only in the geometrical sense, but also in the philosophical sense in which Nietzsche used this concept.[9] We might find ourselves confronting a false choice between the old metaphysical circle or the cybertopological ectoplasm, between the solid sphere where distance is established as a constant surrounding a centre or the teratology of inconsistent figures. As if curvature could not start to vary without falling into indeterminacy.

Let's start with techniques. The value of Euclidean space is paramount, especially for numerically controlled manufacturing. A tool path is fundamentally a parallel to the surface to be manufactured. In other words, a machining program generator starts by calculating the set of points at an equal distance from the surface, distance given by the radius of the spherical tool of the router. A machining program is basically the parallel to a free surface, whichever it is. And the concept of parallel, so fundamental in Euclidean geometry, starts to create interesting problems long before we contemplate free surfaces.

Take all of the decisions that CAD software has to make when it comes to drawing parallels. By definition, the parallel to a point $P$ is the set of points at a given distance from $P$. It is a circle from which we can see that the parallel transforms a figure into another type of figure [fig 1]. In the case of a straight line the parallel is easy to draw as long as we consider the line infinite. In that case the parallels are the two lines transposed on each side of the original line at a given distance. This is the canonical case according to which we generally confuse parallelism and translation [fig 2]. But this misconception can soon be resolved if we consider the finite straight line. There is no surprise as long as we consider the core of the segment whose parallel can be assimilated to the two transposed segments, but what happens at the ends of the line? Rigorously speaking, we must add two half circles to the two segments on each side of the original straight line, because they are indeed at the same given distance from it. In this case the line becomes oblong [fig 3a]. Otherwise, if we want to stick to the intuitive idea of the two segments, we have to add a rule to our definition of the parallel, specifying that we only want the points at a distance that can be determined according to an orthogonal line, meaning where the latter can be calculated [fig 3b]. But we will quickly see that this rule leads us to other problems in the next case – that of the square – since the first result of the parallel will then be eight independent segments [fig 4a].

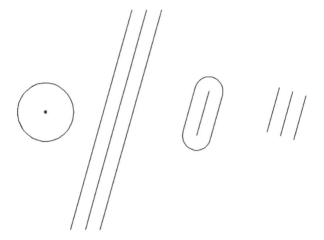

Figure 1, 2, 3a, 3b

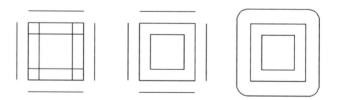

Figure 4a, 4b, 4c

We now have to distinguish the inside of the square from the outside and make two different cases in order to link together the four isolated external segments and shorten the four internal crossing segments. The shortening of the interior segments is preliminary to the elimination of loops in the case of the line above, while the gaps between the four external segments is a direct consequence of our additional rule [fig 4b]. If we cancel this rule again, the external parallel will become a square with rounded corners [fig 4c]. This result might satisfy many people in the moulding industry but it leaves us with a figure different from the original square and its internal parallel. And this would certainly dissatisfy many architects and designers, as well as the primary intuition of the general public. This intuition would tend to extrapolate on the basis of the very special case of the circle, where both the inner and outer parallel remain a shape similar to that of the initial circle [fig 5]. In this case the generation of the parallel creates bigger and smaller circles, and the operation becomes a scaling transformation called *homothétie* in French, after the Greek *homoios,* meaning 'similar'. The dissatisfaction might be even greater when we notice that the parallel is generally not a reciprocal transformation.

If, coming back to our square and its two parallels, we consider the inner one and generate its external parallel at the same distance used previously, we come upon a rounded square, the straight parts of which merge with the sides of the initial square [fig 6]. Thus the reverse parallel of a parallel to an initial figure is not necessarily this initial figure. CAD software usually provides solutions to this problem in the case of orthogonal figures: external parallels can be rounded, squared or chamfered [fig 7].[10] And in the case of architecture software, elements like walls are 'intelligent' enough to behave as the majority would expect them to, which of course can be a serious limitation. Similarly, when figures are composed of more complex elements, CAD software can always find solutions for extrapolating distorted squares, but we must be aware of the irreversible loss of information each time we come

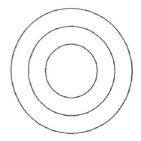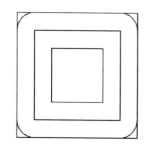

Figure 5, 6

Figure 7

Figure 8

back from an internal parallel to an external parallel [fig 8].

This irreversible loss of information becomes even more blatant in the case of a free, open curve as one increases the distance according to which the parallel is generated. The first effect of the parallel is to reduce the radius of curvature of concavities and increase that of the convexities. This is the case of a positive distance in reference to the concavities, the phenomenon being inverse in the case of a negative distance [fig 9]. The parallel breaks curvature symmetry by emphasising concavity while softening convexity, or vice versa. For architects and designers this isn't just mathematics, since concavity and convexity are the basic intensive qualities on which sculpture is based [fig 10]. As Henry Moore writes, 'Rodin of course knew what sculpture is: he once said that sculpture is the science of the bump and the hollow.'[11] Convexities and concavities are the mathematical equivalents of the sculptural bumps and hollows. But the parallel not only breaks symmetry, it starts creating loops where the distance exceeds the local radius of curvature on the initial curve [fig 11]. The parallel transforms simple undulations into strange but still Euclidean – or should we say, strange *because* Euclidean – figures where loops can themselves include other loops [fig 12]. This too is important for architects and designers, since the basic operation of CAM software cancels the loops on the parallel surface that a spherical tool follows in order to machine a relief. This elimination of loops is responsible for the loss of information that we have already encountered in the case of the square. On the final relief, on the inverse parallel of the parallel, this loss of information will appear as zones where the tool is too large to get into the concavities and will then substitute its own constant radius for the varying curvature of the initial relief [fig 13]. I would bet that baroque architects knew quite a bit about these transformations, which led them to endlessly create curves out of curves, as in the multiplying of cornices and frames.

As one can see, applied Euclidean geometry is not that simple. On examining the intricacies of the basic concept of

parallels on both side of a symmetrical curve

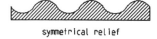

symmetrical relief

convex relief

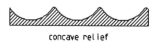

concave relief

Figure 9, 10

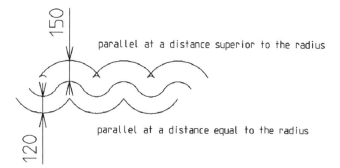

150

parallel at a distance superior to the radius

parallel at a distance equal to the radius

120

Figure II

loops of loops on a parallel to a free curve

machinic parallel

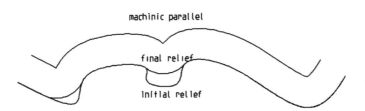

final relief

initial relief

Figure 12, 13

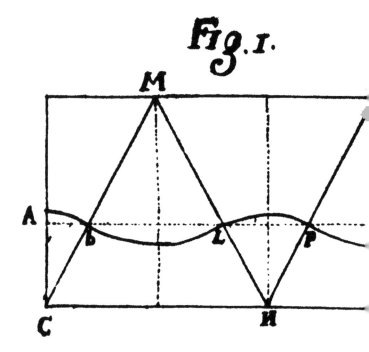

Figure 14

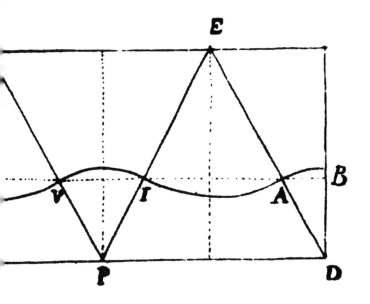

the parallel, it becomes apparent that it is far more complex than the false intuition by which we assimilate parallelism into ordinary transformations such as translation or scaling. There still are very basic operations that the best modellers available on the market, like Parasolid, cannot solve directly. Let us mention, for instance, the generation of a swept shape along a line, the radius of curvature of which becomes locally inferior to half the width of the section. As an example of this type of problem, we would very much like to record the exact geometry of the handrail that Desargues drew for the entrance stairs of the Château de Vizille, built in Dauphiné in 1653, and then check to what extent it can be drawn with current CAD software. What we are hinting at is that architects can turn the complexity of Euclidean geometry into richness. The examination of a simple operation like the parallel of the square produces a variety of unexpected results, but if we think about these difficulties as architects, we can take advantage of them in order to investigate new figures within Euclidean space, figures that we will be able to manufacture and build. At the moment when Euclidean geometry is supported by computers, we can start thinking of the general concept of variable curvature. Circles can be modulated. Parallels no longer need to be drawn at a constant distance. Old methods like Guarini's 'manner of drawing an undulating line' can be pushed further.[12] Figure 14 shows a sketch that Guarini presented in his *Architettura civile*. Arcs of a circle are drawn from the centre, located at the intersection of the oblique lines and passing by the intersection of these oblique lines with a variable horizontal line. Guarini explicitly presents his sketch as a general device that generates a variety of undulating lines; as such, it can be drawn on parametric software. The lines thus generated are more or less concave and convex according to the position of the horizontal line in relation to the middle axis of the rectangle. And if, thanks to the parametric software, you push the horizontal line beyond the limits of the rectangle, you then get the strange looped lines we have already encountered. It is no wonder, since Guarini's sketch is a method for generating undulation by creating parallels at a variable distance. So now think of undulations that don't need to be created out of planar arcs of circles! Think of parallels at a distance that is always variable! Many unexpected figures will then enable us to incarnate complex topologies in Euclidean space.

Originally published in *Any* 24, 1999.

### NOTES

1. See Michel Serres, *Les origines de la géométrie* (Paris: Flammarion, 1993).

2. For architects and designers, it is interesting to notice the logical and geometrical approach to ornament of Jan Hessel de Groot, who restricted himself to generating figures and ornamental motifs using only 45-degree and 60-degree set-squares. His *Dreihoeken bij Ontwerpen van Ornament* [Ornamental Design by Triangles] (Amsterdam: Stemler, 1896) states his aims: 1) to demonstrate the simple way that forms take shape, and their precise self-determination; 2) to provide a tool that can be used to maintain unity in ornamental composition. See Sergio Polano, 'De Groot e l'estetica sistematica', *Casabella* 647.

3. See *Architectura civil* by Juan Caramuel y Lobkowitz, as well as Claude Perrault's critiques of optical corrections.

4. Henri Poincaré, *La science et l'hypothèse* (1902)

5. P. Duhem, 'Dominique Soto et la scolastique parisienne', in *Annales de la Faculté des Lettres de Bordeaux* (Bulletin hispanique, 1911), 454–67.

6. See Wolfgang Lotz, 'Die ovalen Kirchenräume des Cinquecento', in *Architecture in Italy 1500–1600* (New Haven: Yale University Press, 1995).

7. Catia actually bought Euclid while this text was being written.

8. SGDL is now able to handle not only the quadrics, but also the cubics and the quartics.

9. Let us also mention that parallelism was the name under which Leibniz and Spinoza discussed the question of the relation between body and soul.

10. Interestingly enough, we find these three solutions at many architectural scales, starting with the urban block built around a square courtyard. The peripheral contour of the block can remain square or become chamfered (Plan Cerda) or rounded.

11. Henry Moore, *Henry Moore on Sculpture*, edited by Philip James (New York: Da Capo Press, 1992).

12. See Guarino Guarini, 'Del modo di piegare varie linee curve necessarie all'ortografia: maniera di condurre una linea ondeggiante' [How to fold various curved lines necessary for orthography: a way of drawing an undulating line], in *Architettura civile*, III, 3, 2 (Milan: Il Polifilo, 1968).

# TOWARDS A NON-STANDARD
# MODE OF PRODUCTION

Under what conditions does an expression like 'non-standard architecture' have meaning? Perhaps it is easier to begin by saying what it's not. For, if non-standard architecture were to mean generating more or less fluid surfaces which are transferred onto a battery of CAM software in order to qualify as 'buildings' – or rather, very expensive kinds of sculpture that no longer have any relation to the historical and social fabric of the city – then we would merely be perpetuating the romantic myth of the artist–architect. Over and above any polemical intention, this negative introduction should help us to define the criteria that we need to cultivate if we want to exploit the possibilities of a non-standard architecture: at stake are the questions of form, city and productivity.

Let's begin with form, since (why deny it?) this is where the 'fascination' lies. The use of CAD to generate surfaces that generally cannot be designed with ruler and compass instils in architects an extraordinary feeling of power. This feeling of omnipotence may be inspired in the first instance by highly ergonomic programs such as Rhino, which make it easy to create surfaces so complex that one can no longer be certain of their spatial coherence. What the man in the street doesn't know is that this ability – to delineate the control points of a Nurbs surface in order to generate a fluid surface – is now within the reach of any computer user after an apprenticeship of a mere half-hour; and that's how it should be. On the other hand, the ability to then control these surfaces, to modify them by altering their coordinates, to give them a thickness and fabricate them, is a whole new ball game – one that calls for the problems to be passed onto someone else, and for a multiplication of the budget. Hence the adage, oft repeated by lucid architects like Alejandro Zaera Polo: nothing gets built unless it can be transposed onto Autocad.

Then there are the complex generators, such as simulators of particle movements, that we find on graphics software like Maya, Softimage and others. In themselves, these programs cannot be criticised, but they were never intended for fabricating concrete objects, and so are barely concerned with matters such as ensuring that the four corners of a flat board are coplanar, for example. Whereas the appeal of programs like Rhino is related to the simplicity of an extremely transparent interface, here the sense of power comes, on the contrary, from being able to wield tools that are so complex that the means of form-generation are outside our control, so the result materialises as if by magic – a seemingly random or chance occurrence. In this respect the chaos is entirely determinist, but since we don't comprehend the algorithmic determinants, the forms are imprinted with a kind of aura conferred by their alleged randomness.

A third and ultimately much more honest approach is to set aside the computer and simply twist sheets of paper – a time-honoured way of mocking up a sculpture. The advantage of this process is that it creates developable surfaces, ie ones with nil curvature, in other words surfaces that are intrinsically Euclidian.[1] The paper maquette is then digitised so that it can be transferred onto a software program that will regularise its surfaces, before the files are turned over to a specialist in architectural prêt-à-porter, like Permasteelisa.[2]

In these three strategies 'non-standard' is equated with 'original' or 'complex', but in each case we remain entrenched in the Beaux-Arts mentality that treats every architectural project as the opportunity for a work of individual creation. And from this perspective non-standard architecture is inscribed within a tradition of uniqueness that intersects all modes of production – artisanal, artistic, industrial or digital. The alternative viewpoint is the series: the object as a point on a continuum. Yet even here things need to be clarified. Because today we know that anything can be transformed into something else, through the magical workings of morphing. In seeking to avoid the Charybdis of the unique, we soon fall into the Scylla of transformations that lack the consistency that would artificially establish a continuity between otherwise unrelated forms.

*Morphè*, indeed. What is form? What properties must two objects share for them to be considered to have the same form? The answer lies in a concept that is fundamental to architectural theory and geometry alike. Two objects have the same form when, independently of their size, the angles between their elements are the same and, above all, their proportions are consistent. More precisely, the preoccupation with form is fuelled by a theory of proportions that must be clearly grasped if we are to avoid the pitfalls that have ensnared architectural thinking from neo-Pythagorean acoustics to the Modulor of Le Corbusier. And the philosopher who poses the problem most clearly, in relation to architecture, is Plato in the *Sophist*.

Plato is concerned to define the sophists, who professed all things – and the exact opposite – while instructing their pupils in how to overturn any argument in order to defend the contrary thesis. In short, the sophists were image-makers who practised morphing by means of rhetoric. As usual, Plato has Socrates preside over a dialogue where two major positions are examined. One of these, Heraclitus' notion that everything is in motion, is not difficult to reject, because if Being were identical with change, how could we even give a name to the things we speak of? On the other hand, the position of Parmenides seems equally untenable, for he posits that Being is One, necessarily singular and unique. This second thesis is all the more difficult to sustain if we observe Parmenides' famous dichotomy, according to which 'one must Be absolutely, or not at all'. For in this case, what are we to do with the sophists' discourses, which 'are' and yet are at the same time 'false'? In the *Sophist* Plato develops the view that we live in a world where Being and not-Being are entangled. The Greek word is extremely precise: *sumplokê* means 'entanglement' in contexts that extend from the intertwining of bodies in lovemaking or combat to the alternation of vowels and consonants in the formation of words. We live in a world of images and simulacra. The visible world consists merely of copies of Ideas, which are the only entities to escape the cycle of coming-into-being and passing away. Referring specifically to the plastic arts in an architectural context, Plato notes that there are two kinds of copy – on the one hand good copies, which respect the proportions of the model, and on the other simulacra, or shadows and reflections which distort the proportions. The Greek for proportion is *logos*, the Latin *ratio*, which takes us to the very root of rationality and discourse. For Plato every material thing is manifestly corrupted by its coming-into-being, to the extent that no physical model can equal the *eidôs*, the Idea or Form. The perfect relationship, in Plato, is the one that will convert identity into an ideal proportion: the isometric relationship of sameness, the ratio of 1:1.

Today we have everything we need to construct a philosophy of the image which certainly could not have been envisaged in Plato's time, but which nonetheless responds to the philosopher's requirements. Forms, those abstract entities, are invariants that escape corruption. In the first rank we find identity, the relationship of sameness which enables the thing to be superimposed upon the image, or rest upon movement. The same goes for those perfect forms, the circle or the sphere, which remain identical to themselves in the movement of rotation around their centre. In rotating invariants the same measurements are preserved. Next, we have those somewhat degraded copies that reproduce the model while altering its dimensions. These copies remain 'good', however, in as much as the painter, sculptor or architect has respected the correct proportions of the model. The result: 'similitudes' preserving both angles and proportions, where the ratio is invariant through homothety (similarity). The shadow of the pyramid varies depending on the hour, day and season, but the relationship of the pyramid to its shadow remains identical to the relationship between the gnomon planted in the ground and its own shadow – these relationships are invariants by variation, entanglements of being and becoming. Plato holds his fire here, reserving his main attack for those sculptors who alter the proportions of statues placed on temple acroteria in order to compensate for optical deformations (the apparent angle of the different superimposed parts changes very quickly when statues are seen from below, in perspective). With this, we enter the realm of perspectival manipulations reprised by Vitruvius and subsequently taken up in numerous architectural treatises. But we should take care here. Plato does not question the reason for these manipulations. His attitude is very different to that of Claude Perrault, say, who as a good Cartesian would categorically reject the idea that our senses could be deceived – a circle would always be perceived as a circle, even though its apparent profile is an ellipse when viewed from an angle. And damn people like Caramuel y Lobkowitz, who wanted to deform the section of the colonnade of St Peter's in Rome so as to take account of its perspectival deformation. Cartesian rationalism holds firmly to this rejection of the hypothesis of the evil genius. In this respect, there is a total incompatibility between Descartes and Desargues, who both produced their seminal texts just before 1640. And we might also want to consider whether there is not an equally wide gulf separating the two great projective geometers, Desargues and Pascal, for whereas Desargues treated the vanishing point as an ordinary point, Pascal developed it into a mystique of the infinite.[3] This splintering of French rationalist philosophy around 1640 was tied, not so much to the 'zeitgeist', as to divergent strands at the core of so-called 'classical' thinking.

But let's get back to Plato, who recognised there were valid theoretical reasons for optical corrections – but objected to the practical results. A statue placed above a column has to be distorted, yet this copy with altered

proportions is the very prototype of the simulacra that
Plato attacked. The mathematics of the time did not have
the means to conceive of Forms that remain invariant
through projective transformations. To see something
other than deformation or corruption, Plato would have
needed to have had access to projective invariants, and
in particular the biratio, that relationship of relationships
which is preserved in projective deformations. We can see,
too, how the discourse of science proceeds. The primitive
invariant is the relationship of identity, an isometric
relationship of sameness. Next comes the second kind
of invariance by variation, the homothetic relationship –
an expression of Greek rationality that we do not take
our leave of till 1639, at least in terms of its translation
to geometrical space. Desargues now makes his entrance,
followed closely by Pascal, the two of them creating
the first geometrical projective invariants, alignment and
intersection, prior to the invention of the numerical
birational. Following Desargues, another 100 years would
elapse before the invention of the first topological invariants, which are preserved through surface deformations
of any kind, insofar as their continuity is respected. Euler's
famous formula of 1736 opened up an area of investigation
that is far from exhausted: the theory of invariants charac-
terising knots remains a very active subject of research in
contemporary mathematics.[4] But it was ultimately Felix
Klein who in 1872 formulated a theory that allowed for the
invention of increasingly sophisticated invariants, enabling
us to manipulate ever-greater variations.[5]

What relation can this very brief sketch of the history
of geometry have with the opportunities we have, right
now, to create an architecture that is genuinely non-
standard? To begin with, we can retain an altogether
classical definition of architecture: the ordering of space
in such a manner as to ensure the greatest possible freedom
for the people who collectively frequent or colonise it.
Ordering means equipping a space that is not naturally
habitable with fixed points (invariants) and a means
of orientation, for absolute space, without any kind of

structure, is scarcely more inhabitable than the hyper-grid of a totalitarian architecture. We need to find mediating devices that will ensure a supple variety in the necessary invariants, since between absolute variation and total invariance there is room for a whole spectrum of invariants by variation. Which brings us to a non-standard architecture: the notion may not be completely new in itself, but digital technologies may enable us to cross a threshold into new territory. Putting aside the extremes of form created with isometric invariants (such as Newton's cenotaph or the concentrated spaces of Hilberseimer), architectural thinking has always emphasised proportional invariants. Even when attempting to elaborate a universal system of industrial standardisation, Le Corbusier still went back to proportion. That he then invoked a harmonic, neo-Pythagorean concept dreamt up by nineteenth-century German ideologues does not in any way diminish the relevance of the idea of proportion in architecture; on the contrary, this modern error proves just how difficult it is to conceive of architecture without proportion. Moreover, whenever the theorists of the Italian Renaissance attempted to interpret the perspective system invented by Brunelleschi in 1420, they still returned to the system of proportions, striving (in vain) to drape the projective over the similitude by establishing simple ratios between the diminishing segments of a paved area seen in perspective, even though this is a classic case of the projective biratio.

The fact is that architecture has always had a highly ambiguous relation to projective geometry, even though it was architects who first laid the groundwork for and then invented this geometry – in a process that spans over 200 years, from Brunelleschi to Desargues via Philibert de l'Orme, and extends at least as far as Monge, who first used it in the military fortifications at the École Mézières. And even though architects were the ones who plotted the projective coordinates, the stereotomic works incorporating this geometry always remained secondary – at best, we have the magnificent vaults in the Hôtel de Ville in Arles;[6] much more typical are simple additions such as the squinches used by Philibert de l'Orme. And the role of topological invariants, strapwork and the like, appears even more problematic, with the knot or foliated scroll acting as a basic ornamental motif,[7] a register from which – until very recently – they have hardly ever deviated, aside from a few specific applications such as the extraordinary staircases created by Philibert de l'Orme for the Château d'Anet.[8]

This formal analysis of course needs to be refined, but the more we consider the history of architecture from the CAD-CAM angle, the more it seems to us that tradition has always integrated, albeit in varying doses, these four types of invariant: isometric, homothetic, projective and topological. What is different today is that we now have the means to challenge the implicit system of hierarchy between these different registers and to develop more sophisticated invariants, both projective and topological. Regular polygons such as the Tower of the Winds, the first building described in Vitruvius' *De Architectura,* hardly raise an eyebrow anymore. On the other hand, urban power relations have seriously called into question the proportions of classical architecture. Yet we have no faith in a merely topological architecture – aleatory, fluid, moving or virtual, wrongly labelled non-Euclidian – any more than we once believed in an isometric architecture that was central, orthogonal and panoptic. Rather, what we're aiming at is a means of integrating the different registers of invariants as an alternative to the solution promoted by the current media consensus – spatial hernias in a few privileged locations in the urban centres, and unchecked chaos/ gridification in the suburbs. In general, putting aside the cases where certain invariants are defined by the context of the building itself, architecture is better able to order the diversity of space when it brings each of the four registers of invariant into play, deterritorialising their traditional field of application – the isometry of the central plan, the similitude of a proportional architectonics, the projectivity of complex solids, and the topology of intertwining ornaments. This reinterpretation of traditional registers involves a rereading of historical urban typologies. An architecture based on variable invariants provides an alternative way to approach typology than the neo-Platonist mode of the identically or proportionally reproducible model.[9] The city becomes a testbed for the varying of historical invariants.

This raises a number of questions. Since urban relationships are determined, at least in part, by the relations of production, how do we ensure that a non-standard architecture becomes a true social fact rather than a luxury item for a well-heeled clientele? How do we prevent the non-standard from collapsing into original formalism? How can we guarantee that the object will be genuinely conceived and produced as a single instance in a series? How do we integrate the architectural object into the urban fabric? To all these questions there is, in our opinion, one basic response: the productivity of the various agencies of architecture, with conception keeping pace with fabrication. From this point of view, the question of non-standard architecture is no different from the basic problem of postindustrial societies, namely the productivity of services in general.[10] The architect is an intellectual worker whose mode of production is conditioned by digital technologies, but these hardly develop along natural lines. Thus the writing of software programs is at the same time the main genre of contemporary culture and the privileged terrain for confronting the forces that organise production in our societies.[11] In this regard, there is one strategic concept that will determine the form that standard architecture will take in the years ahead – the concept of associativeness.

What are we to understand by this term? Associativeness is the principle used in software that organises the architectural project in a long chain of relationships, from the first conceptual ideas to the driving of the machines that will prefabricate the components to be assembled on site. Designing on an associative software program comes down to transforming the geometrical design into a programming language interface. Thus, creating a point at the intersection of two lines no longer requires the creation

**68**

of a graphic element, but rather the establishment of a relationship of intersection on the basis of two relations of alignment. The reader will recall that this involves two basic projective invariants – intersection and alignment – as well as two primitive gestures in space: aiming and intercepting. The whole point of associative CAD-CAM software programs is to translate this geometrical relationship into a program to ensure that the point of intersection is correctly recalculated when we displace the end-points of the line segments that we intersect. Of course, this is merely an elementary link; all this only has architectural interest if we are able to set up long sequences of subordinates on the basis of a small number of primitive elements called, in the technical jargon, 'original parents'. The first consequence of associativeness is therefore the need to give the architectural project a formal rationalisation, taking great care to distinguish antecedents from dependents, so as not to create circular references or other logical incongruities. Associativeness therefore constitutes a filter obliging us to think through the architectural project in a rational way and to define its hypotheses. This ought to encourage clear thinking in both the processes and the concepts of architecture – which makes it all the more surprising that it has aroused so little interest among those who used to proclaim themselves exponents of a rational architecture.

What we have just described relates only to the active conception of the project. But the whole difficulty of non-standard architecture lies in the sheer quantity of data that has to be generated and manipulated in order to industrially fabricate components that are totally different to each other at a cost no greater than standardised production. In order to manage these data flows and guarantee that conception and fabrication are fully integrated, it is essential to work on the same nucleus so that we can, among other things, control the dimensions of the components from the conception stage right up to the writing of the ISO code programs for the digital machines driving the production of the objects. For these reasons, the technical specifications for such a CAD-CAM associative system include at least four basic elements. The first of these responds to the need to handle vast groups of complex elements, all of them different, which can no longer be designed individually. This calls for a process known in technical terms as the 'insertion of components', which begins with the devising of a 'model' of relation that can be applied in all the situations in which a component of this type needs to be created. This model is in some respects an invariant that has to accommodate all the variations undergone by the terms that we have established relations between. That platonism contains the seeds of all these technological developments in our Western societies is a statement that need no longer be the subject or speculation or theorisation, for it is verified empirically by our professional practice. And in our experience, too, the implementation of this logic of components in a non-standard project has the potential to increase productivity a hundredfold! It is in the specific context of productivity gains of this magnitude that the term 'non-standard architecture' acquires real meaning.

Another aspect of the technical specifications is the need to work in extended flux, with information remaining provisional – and delocalised – right up to the very last moment. It was Moholy-Nagy who said in the 1920s that the criterion of the modernity of a work was its ability to be transmitted by telephone. This principle applies even more today. The multiplicity of collaborators, their geographical dispersal, the volatility of decisions, all oblige us to begin formalising the project on the basis of uncertain information. We have to be able to give default values, amending them as required; define points in a geometric location without specifying a definitive position; and bring manufacturing programs up to date the day before their implementation. Prior to taking shape as constructed buildings, non-standard architecture proceeds from an abstract architecture that orders the flow of data necessary for digital production, and in a more automated way, since there is no longer an intermediary between designer and machine. Any modification of one of the original parents of the project has to automatically set in motion the updating of the entire sequence of information, because human intervention is always subject to error. As it is, a truly non-standard architecture will only emerge if it is able to reproduce in the realm of construction what has already occurred in publishing. In the same way that an author can now write and lay out a graphic document and put it online, where it can be accessed and printed on demand by a distant reader, so non-standard architecture presupposes that the designer of a building is capable of producing all the documents required for the distant production of architectural components, without the need for any regulatory authority or quantity surveyor to filter out the errors. Lastly, if we want this to move beyond the utopian stage, the automated sequence of data must include the documents that support the economic transactions necessary to the production of the structure: specifications, estimate, production and delivery orders, assembly plans, etc.

To be sure, all these technical specifications turn associativeness into a mechanism that is at once very powerful and very complex. CAD-CAM software is only just beginning to implement this kind of approach in spheres such as mechanics. There is nothing to suggest that this full and entire associativeness will remain forever limited to highly specialised, defined industrial applications. But if we want it to be inscribed within economic reality – raised above the level of mere technological prowess – then we need to firmly integrate conception and production. Indeed, what is the point of developing highly sophisticated software unless the people who use it – and architects, in particular – are interested in how it works and in exploiting its potential to the full? What use is it, either, to develop an associativeness between conception and fabrication if in practice manufacturers and clients fail to establish relationships enabling them to make the most of the continuity of the flow of information? Until the two parties define a way of working that favours collaboration, rather than a set up where they can artificially break this chain and pin the blame on the other party, associativeness will be a mere software-producer's marketing ploy, or worse still, a strategic development error. Now, more than ever, we need to progressively and patiently construct a genuine culture of digital production if architecture is to benefit from the opportunities offered by the non-standard.

Originally published in Bernard Leupen, René Heijne, Jasper van Zwol (eds.), *Time-based Architecture* (Rotterdam: 010 Publishers, 2005).

## NOTES

1. On all surfaces developable on a plane, the sum of the angles of a triangle remains constant and equals 180°.

2. An Italian company that is the market leader in claddings for large, irregularly shaped buildings.

3. It is important to note that the theorem of the mystical hexagon was conceived long before Pascal had any connection with Port-Royal, the Jansenist convent that his sister entered, and was therefore a mystical process of his own invention. Was Guarini, who rejected the secular implications of Arguesian geometry, aware of this?

4. Euler's formula is V-E+F=2: for any convex polyhedron, the number of vertices and faces combined is exactly two more than the number of edges.

5. Felix Klein expounded his general conceptions of geometry in his text, *Über die sogenannte nicht-euklidische Geometrie* (1871).

6. Probably built by Hardouin-Mansart around 1640.

7. See Gottfried Semper, *Der Stil*, 1861 and Alois Riegl, *Stilfragen* (1893).

8. See the reconstruction drawing in Philippe Potié, *Philibert De L'Orme, Figures de la pensée constructive* (Marseilles: ed Parenthèses, 1991).

9. At the level of problems, platonist philosophy seems much more open than most of its later interpreters would have us believe.

10. See Paul R Krugman, *The Age of Diminished Expectations* (Cambridge, MA: MIT Press, 1990) and 'Pop Internationalism', *Economic Perspectives* 1:2 (1997).

11. We would like to express our gratitude here to those at Missler who are continuing to develop the TopSolid software program on which the Objectile application is based – and above all to Christian Arber, Jean-Luc Rolland and their whole team of collaborators, including Jean-Louis Jammot and Charles Claeys.

# GEOMETRIES OF *PHÀNTASMA*[1]

**The main task of a translator of the *Sophist* is the following: convince the reader that any clear, absolutely comprehensible and, indeed, elegant translation of this dialogue is necessarily unfaithful to the original. For, ever since antiquity, the *Sophist* has been considered one of Plato's most obscure texts.**

This is the tenor of Néstor-Luis Cordero's warning to readers at the outset of a dialogue that he also describes as a 'posterior course', that is to say a thorough revamping of the system that had previously been elaborated in Plato's key work, the *Republic*. I am therefore well aware of the risks involved when I attempt another translation of the *Sophist*, one employing a different kind of language, namely geometry or, more exactly, geometry in its reciprocal relationship to architecture.

**Let no one ignorant of geometry enter here.**

Geometry occupied a very special place in Plato's world: it was the pivot between the visible and the invisible, between the sensible and the intelligible. On the one hand, geometry played a propaedeutic role by showing how we must detach ourselves from the sensorial and specific in order to focus on the intellectual; geometers gaze upon the figures before their eyes only in order to contemplate the intelligible Forms that are the real object of knowledge of true Being. Yet on the other hand, in the basic scheme of the *Republic*, geometry constitutes only the lower level of the intelligible world. More precisely, geometry and the other sciences are called 'hypothetical', and for that reason they cannot lead us to knowledge of essential things. 'There

are two subdivisions [of the intelligible domain], in the
lower of which the soul uses the figures given by the
former division as images; the enquiry can only be
hypothetical, and instead of going upwards to a principle
descends [downward to a conclusion]' (*Republic* VI: 510b).[2]

Plato was very clearly aware – as were, in a more
general way, Aristotle and other Greek thinkers who strove
to define the status of logical systems such as geometry –
of the impossibility of relying on exclusively rational
foundations, and therefore of the need to resort to
postulates. Whether the term 'hypothesis' be taken in the
sense of an axiom or in the sense of a simple working
premise, or whether we shift back and forth between these
meanings to create a kind of axiomatic–dialectic synthesis,
as Socrates did in *Meno*[3] – virtue sometimes being
goodness (a postulate accepted by all, yet indemonstrable)
and sometimes being knowledge that can be taught (an
arbitrary hypothesis subject to debate) – the realm of
hypothesis bears the mark of everything that cannot be
grounded in *logos* alone, which explains Plato's need to
call on a second level of the intelligible, said to be above
hypothesis, or 'nonhypothetical'. Thus in the second part
of *Parmenides*, when Zeno joins Socrates to ask Parmenides
to demonstrate the method he advocates, the philosopher
from Elea does so by admitting that he must begin by
formulating a hypothesis, 'if one exists', but that it would
also be appropriate to examine the inverse consequences
'if one does not exist' (*Parmenides*, 137b). Hypothesis is
therefore subject to denial. Later, in the *Posterior Analytics*,
Aristotle would constantly assert that principles cannot be
demonstrated. Employing demonstrative reasoning alone,
a proposition such as 'the sum of the angles of a triangle
equals 180°' remains one hypothesis among others and
can only be salvaged at the very end of the *Analytics* (11: 19)
by recourse to intuition. Taking this sum as an object of
*logos* alone means that everything and its opposite can be
asserted, which is precisely typical of the mode of
argument adopted by the sophists. Hence the discourse
that, once systematised by Euclid, would embody the very

model of rationality for the subsequent 21 centuries, opened the door to sophistry. Which required Plato to react at the level of first principles.

How, indeed, could a sophist be defined? Plato did so progressively, adopting no fewer than six definitions before reaching the heart of the problem. He successively defines a sophist as:

> a hunter of rich youths for their wealth
> a trader in learned things ('goods of the soul')
> a retailer of learned things
> a manufacturer of learned things
> a professional disputer
> a purger of souls.

At this point, the 'Stranger' who is orchestrating the dialogue pauses before introducing a shift in the debate. 'I should imagine', he says, that sophists 'are supposed to have knowledge of those things about which they dispute … And therefore, to their disciples, they appear to be all-wise?' Yet someone who claims to know all and teach all must also be an entertainer, and the most technical and most pleasant form of entertainment is imitation. A sophist thereby becomes a maker of spoken images – an imitator.

Now what, exactly, is an image? There are several kinds. Natural images are reflections seen in the water, or shadows cast by the sun. Artificial images are the paintings and statues seen at the tops of temples. In all cases, an image is the duplicate of a model, but this duplication may be duplicated in two ways depending on its relationship to the original. On the one hand there are copies that respect the original proportions of the model in terms of length, width and depth. And then there are monumental works where the proportions of the original model are altered, because otherwise 'the upper part, which is farther off, would appear to be out of proportion in comparison with the lower, which is nearer' (*Sophist*, 236a). Whereas the first type of image merits the name of copy, the other type is described as *phàntasma*, which Néstor-Luis Cordero translates as *illusion*. The main thing to grasp is that while a good copy requires respect for proportions, illusions are not necessarily invalid. They are clearly the product of alterations, but such optical correction is required to save appearances, given the growing decrease in apparent angle as the monumental statues rise higher and higher. It is on the basis of the validity of illusion that the Stranger poses the question that will then become central:

**We are engaged in a very difficult speculation – there can be no doubt of that; for how a thing can appear and seem, and not be, or how a man can say a thing which is not true? This has always been and still remains a very perplexing question. Can anyone say or think that falsehood really exists, and avoid being caught in a contradiction?**
(*Sophist*, 336e)

The problem of sophistry thus comes to hinge on the 'Being' or 'not-Being' of images. If an image is only an illusion, pure not-Being, how can sophists be accused of falsehoods, since falsehoods do not really exist? An image must claim a minimum of Being if the charges against the sophists are to have any substance. But if an image is something, then are sophists not expressing something that has Being and is therefore true?

This brings us to the relationship between Being and not-Being. On one side there were the 'friends of Form' (*eidôs philos*) – the disciples of Parmenides, as Plato himself long remained. For them, Being is univocal: Being is, and Being is One. Not-Being is not. Images, bodies, tangible things, movement: all of them are mere appearance. The only truth is the stable, invariant Being that is the very foundation of all organised discourse, because how could we say anything about something that is constantly shifting? The same applies to the very possibility of naming things.

On the other side there were the 'friends of matter' (*gêgênes*). They recognised only material, physical, sensory and changing reality. Homer himself asserted that the soul, that is to say the seat of intellect, was the power that set the body in motion.

The Stranger in the *Sophist* criticises both sides equally. Against the friends of matter he maintains what Plato always argued, namely the need to seek invariant Forms among the shifting appearances of phenomena. Against the friends of Form, meanwhile, he objects that there is no knowledge without a subject who knows, and who is therefore affected or moved. And being moved inevitably implies change.

As is so well summed up by Cordero, in the realm of knowledge an object presupposes rest whereas a subject – which is intellect, and therefore soul, and therefore life – introduces motion. We thus need to establish a link between rest and movement, and to conceive of a total Being that encompasses these different realities. This total Being, which will jointly host error and illusion as well as the most stable of Forms, is a minimum Being, a power to act and to be affected, however minimally:

**My notion would be, that anything which possesses any sort of power [*dunamis*] to affect another, or to be affected by another, if only for a single moment, however trifling the cause and however slight the effect, has real existence; and I hold that the definition of Being is simply power [*dunamis*].** (*Sophist*, 247e)

This extraordinary definition of Being as a minimal power to act or be affected has certain Spinozist or Nietzschean overtones. Plato/the Stranger goes on to say that this power links motion to rest, not in an indiscriminate fashion – because movement would then totally stop and rest would, in turn, be in motion – but rather via a classification of Forms that weaves one into the other.

Classifying rest and motion, invariance and variation, is precisely what a 24-year-old mathematician suggested 21 centuries later when attempting to reorganise the edifice of geometry. That edifice was then cracking under a double strain:

on the one hand there were geometries that assigned values other than 180° to the sum of the angles of a triangle;[4]

on the other hand there were geometries – led by projective geometry, later relayed by topology – that sought to describe space without concern for measurements.

That mathematician was Felix Klein, best known to the general public for his strange bottle with no distinct inside or outside. On his appointment to a teaching post in 1872, Klein gave an inaugural address now famously known as the Erlangen Programme (see table below). His idea was to reconceive the architecture of geometry by distinguishing several levels, each structured by properties that remain invariant under a characteristic transformation.

*The architecture of geometry according to the Erlangen Programme (1872)*

| Geometry | Characteristic transformation | Geometric invariant | Numerical invariant |
|---|---|---|---|
| Isometry | Rotation | Distances (identity) | Number $a_1 = a_2$ |
| Similarity | Homothetic | Angles (form) Ratio | $(a_1/b_1 = (a_2/b_2)$ |
| Projective | Projection | Intersection and alignment | Cross ratio $[(a_1/b_1)/(c_1/d_1)]$ $= [(a_2/b_2)/(c_2/d_2)]$ |
| Topology | Deformation | Continuity | More complex relationships (eg the Euler number): $V + F - E$ |

The table is designed to provide an extremely simplified version of the architecture of geometry as conceived by Felix Klein. The number of geometries has been reduced to four, each characterised by a transformation that leaves numerical and geometric properties invariant.

It should be remembered that this programme was proposed in 1872. When Plato wrote the *Sophist* in 370 BCE he had only two types of invariant at his disposal: lengths and angles on the one hand, and proportions on the other. Geometry, which would soon be developed into a formal system by Euclid, was above all a system of measurement combined with a theory of proportions. It was a two-level geometry, so when Plato sought to reconcile rest and motion he had only a very limited number of invariants to hand. At the level of isometry, the perfect figure was the one that maintained invariant lengths and enjoyed the possibility of sphere of the superlunary world. At the level of similarity, the figure of invariance by variation was given by the conjunction of the shadows of gnomon and pyramid, shadows that constantly vary yet whose ratio (*logos*, or proportion) remains constant.

Hence this distinction between images – between those that retain proportions on the one hand and those that alter them on the other. With the *Sophist*, Plato pulled off a major coup. While all the while subscribing to the theory of proportions – as would Vitruvius and subsequently all theories of art and architecture – which represented the most highly evolved invariant of classical science, Plato simultaneously recognised the existence of projective deformations and dared to accord them incontrovertible reality. The Stranger in no way contests the need to deform monumental statues; he would probably have agreed to Juan Caramuel y Lobkowitz's ovalisation of the sections of the columns in his counter-proposal for St Peter's Square in Rome. Yet recognising the projective field was completely contrary to the neoclassical attitude of, say, Claude Perrault, who denied the utility of perspectival manipulations, arguing that a circle is always *perceived* as

a circle, even when viewed from an angle; indeed, since
all Cartesian thought was grounded in the rejection of
the hypothesis of the evil genius, the possibility of
misleading the senses was a major risk for *any* philosophy
based on evidence.

What do we mean by recognition of projective
deformations? We certainly do not mean that Plato foretold
or already entertained the concepts that underlie projective
geometry. Neither the optical corrections made by ancient
architects nor the perspective drawings made by Brunelleschi could lay claim to projective conceptualisation in the
strict sense of the term. When Alberti wrote his *Ludi
mathematici* ('Mathematical Games') he limited himself
to applications of the theorem of similar triangles. This
led to the thorny question of the law of the foreshortening
of intercolumniation in perspective depictions of porticoes,
which remained a troubling issue as long as the answer
was sought in terms of proportion. On the level of concepts,
there indeed occurred a rupture – a double rupture,
even – with the arrival of Girard Desargues followed by
Brook Taylor. The key event was Desargues' *Brouillon*
('Rough Draft') project of 1639. The French architect
considered points at infinity exactly like ordinary points,
which allowed him not only to handle cylindrical and
conic projections in the same fashion, but also to assimilate
various conic sections to a single and unique curve.
Nevertheless, as Rudolf Bkouche has stressed, 'Desargues'
demonstrations respected Greek tradition, and they remain
based on the theory of proportions'.[5] It was not until 1715,
when Taylor wrote his *Linear Perspective, or a New Method
of Representing Justly All Manners of Objects as They Appear
to the Eye in All Situations*, that we finally disposed of
demonstrations based exclusively on projective properties,
namely properties of incidence.

What date, then, should we ascribe to the advent of
a projective approach? The year 1639, when the first
concepts were invented, or 1715, when demonstrations were
completely freed from the theory of proportions? Indeed,
the process of emergence might even be extended up to the

moment when Arthur Cayley (1821–1895) formulated a projective geometry that no longer relied on any metric notion. In the other direction, perhaps we should not overlook the Hellenistic theorems of Menelaus (70–130 CE) and Pappus (290–350 CE), which already bore on projective concepts. Nothing could be more dangerous than trying to reduce historical temporality to simple and exclusive models, such as epistemological breaks versus genealogical continuity. On the contrary, we need to elaborate complete models that allow us to conceive continuity and rupture jointly, along with the contemporary and the anachronistic, and with progress and repetition. Such models already exist: we need merely think of percolation thresholds and catastrophe theory, which are perhaps only in their initial stages. Whatever the case, it is useful to distinguish between facts and concepts. Indeed, determining a scientific fact is always a creative act and may, as such, be challenged independently of any conceptual elaboration. Singling out one phenomenon within diversity and recognising it as a significant fact even though it upsets the current state of knowledge is already an act of invention. That Plato took monumental statues into consideration, that he did not reject them as artistically bizarre, that he recognised the validity of their deformation as a function of a changing angle of vision – a deformation that violated the theory of proportions – would appear to be a positive step that erects a projective approach into a problematic issue, although one devoid, as it would remain for a long time, of any conceptual articulation.

The positive nature of Plato's contribution may emerge more clearly if we compare it to negative approaches or practices lacking all value. I have already mentioned the case of Perrault who, even after Desargues had formulated the first projective concepts, denied the relevance of optical correction in the constitution of the architectural orders.[6] But the role of the determination, or denial, of facts in the realm of science has also been striking in the field of biology. Stephen Jay Gould has pointed out that most biologists in the early nineteenth century already thought that adaptation and natural selection played a major role in the development of species; Darwin's major coup resulted from his reliance on that mechanism alone, rejecting all other approaches such as Lamarck's vitalism. The progressive selection of totally random variations, completely devoid of directionality, sufficed to explain the evolution of species. And Darwin proclaimed this without knowing any of the mechanisms of heredity later discovered by Mendel, which meant that he developed his theory without being able to expound the mechanisms of genetic mutation that drive it. Furthermore, Darwin fully pursued this path even though he was aware that certain features were hard to interpret in terms of natural selection. Chapter 6 of *On the Origin of Species* was precisely titled 'Difficulties on Theory'. There he wrote:

**This is the most interesting department of natural history, and may be said to be its very soul. What can be more curious than that the hand of a man, formed for grasping, that of a mole for digging, the leg of the horse, the paddle of the porpoise, and the wing of the bat, should all be constructed on the same pattern, and should include the same bones in the same proportions.**

Darwin was therefore well aware of this fact, which assumed fundamental significance for the structuralist disciples of Geoffroy Saint-Hilaire, who would later be proven partly correct by DNA biology.[7] But Darwin managed to constitute his theory of evolution thanks to a determined elimination of all facts other than the selection of tiny, random variations, even if that meant acknowledging difficulties that would have to be resolved at a later date.

Returning to the Plato of the *Sophist*, our Greek philosopher was obviously a long way from inventing anything remotely resembling a projective concept. On the other hand, by accepting the deformation of proportions of statues as a pertinent approach, he was able to elaborate, through his theory of minimal Being, a list of requirements that corresponds quite well to the current theory of invariants by variation:

**Then the philosopher, who has the truest reverence for these qualities, cannot possibly accept the notion of those who say that the whole is at rest, either as unity or in many forms: and he will be utterly deaf to those who assert universal motion. As children say entreatingly 'Give us both', so he will include both the moveable and immoveable in his definition of Being and All.**
(*Sophist*, 249c–d)

Finding a way to articulate precisely the two most contrary notions of motion and rest thus became the central point of the dialogue. 'Alas, Theaetetus, methinks that we are now only beginning to see the real difficulty of the enquiry.'

Though Plato obviously lacked the means to construct a true theory of invariants by variation, he nevertheless tried hard to articulate one. All that he managed to express was the need to choose between three possibilities of linkage or intercommunication, only *one* of which was necessary. 'For, surely, either all things have communication with all; or nothing with any other thing; or some things communicate with some things and others not.' Aware of the difficulty of establishing a general theory that satisfied his requirements, Plato/the Stranger employed an example:

**This communication of some with some may be illustrated by the case of letters; for some letters do not fit each other, while others do … And the vowels, especially, are a sort of bond which pervades all the other letters, so that without a vowel one consonant cannot be joined to another.** (*Sophist*, 253a-b)

Words intertwine, braided together so that vowels and consonants have countervailing values. Here we find again the notion that Plato had already used in order to recognise that the image illusion was a not-Being that is. 'In what a strange complication of Being and not-Being we are involved! ... See how, by his reciprocal [complications], the many-headed sophist has compelled us, quite against our will, to admit the existence of not-Being' (*Sophist*, 240c).

The key word here is the Greek term *sumplokê*, which means complication, interlinkage or 'entanglement' in contexts as varied as wrestling, sexual relationships, the combining of letters to form words, and of words themselves to form propositions. But Plato/the Stranger was developing a theory of discourse in which a noun was to 'rest' what a verb is to 'motion': 'A succession of nouns only is not a sentence, any more than of verbs without nouns' (*Sophist*, 262a). Hence discourse is no longer a matter of *logos*, that is to say proportion, *ratio*, pure reason, but rather of *sumplokê*. In other words Plato, lacking the means to elaborate either a specific theory of projective invariants or a general theory of geometric invariants as a whole, takes as epistemological models the objects that would later pertain to another level of geometry, namely topology. Plato did not build the edifice of geometry, but he explored its different levels.

Unable to formulate a theory of invariants in intension, Plato does so in extension. Sphere and interlacing are extreme figures: isometry on the one hand, topology on the other. From the standpoint of invariance, a sphere is a maximal figure whereas an interlacing is a figure so minimal that its formalisation is still beyond us.[8] Plato's strength was the ability to explore the various degrees of Being-power in both directions, the way a musician can run up and down scales. On the one hand, the major system of the *Republic* and *Timaeus* culminates with spherical perfection as an affirmation of the maximal invariant; on the other, the minor system of the *Sophist* listens to the variations of a minimal Being that takes the form of entangled linkage. Already in *Parmenides*, Plato had been led to contemplate the need to recognise a certain reality to every Being, however minimal: 'such things as hair, mud, dirt, or anything else which is vile and paltry' (*Parmenides*, 130c).

Via geometry, however, it is really the general form of discourse and thought that is at stake. Thinking means not only identifying and proportioning, it also means projecting and interlinking.[9] The *Sophist* removes discourse from the sole governance of *logos*, and all the more so from its extreme form of the identity-ratio of 1:1. This, I would wager, is what encouraged Plato constantly to entangle *mythos* and *logos* in his *Dialogues*,[10] dichotomous logic no longer providing sufficient foundation for his principles. And this entangled yet rigorous form of discourse is what Plato wanted to produce at the opening and closing of the *Sophist*.

Indeed, far from being just a simple, introductory ploy, the opening set of definitions of a sophist should be taken very seriously, because it supplies us with a formal schema that authorises a shift from dichotomy to entanglement. For as long as we stick with the two initial definitions, that of the angler, or fisherman, and the first one given for the sophist, we remain within a normal case of logical branching. When it comes to 'an understanding not only about the name of the angler's art, but about the definition of the thing itself', successive dichotomies were invoked to demonstrate that:

one half of all art was acquisitive – half of the acquisitive art was conquest or taking by force, half of this was hunting, and half of hunting was hunting animals, half of this was hunting water animals – of this again, the under half was fishing, half of fishing was striking: a part of striking was fishing with a barb, and one half of this again, being the kind which strikes with a hook and draws the fish from below upwards, is the art which we have been seeking, and which from the nature of the operation is denoted angling or drawing up (*aspalieutike, anaspasthai*).

The length of this somewhat artificial series of logical operations may seem droll, especially once we realise that this same chain will be repeated six times. Faced with a long list of basic, reiterated operations, modern readers will

not only laugh but will immediately think of an algorithmic
coding process whose structure should be grasped.
From the angler Plato then moves to the sophist: both are
hunters, though they do not go after the same game.
He reminds the reader that hunting had already been
subdivided into 'hunting after swimming animals and
[hunting after] land animals.' Swimming game versus
walking game: the point of the dichotomy is clearly
signalled by the two diverging branches of the tree that
ultimately lead to anglers at one extremity and sophists
at the other.

At this stage of the division process (*Sophist*, 226c), a
separating technique makes it possible to 'card' the series
of basic operations. Carding, spooling and spinning are
weaving analogies applied to the dichotomies designed to
clearly separate the threads. Yet immediately after this first
definition of the sophist, the exact opposite occurs. We
retain the points of division from which the threads
diverge, but their divergence is merely temporary; the six
definitions of the sophist ultimately converge on the same
object. So on the one hand these definitions challenge the
application of the method, since the point of dichotomy
appears to be totally arbitrary – why branch off here rather
than elsewhere? – but ultimately it is the method itself that
is challenged since in the final analysis the threads, initially
separated, are knotted together again. Dichotomous
branching did not suffice to define a sophist, so the logical
method was changed. From logical tree we first shifted to a
bundle of threads knotted at both ends. But this strictly
linear logic would also have to be dropped in order to
develop a new, tabulated one – the one that concludes the
dialogue in the final definition of a sophist, where Plato/the
Stranger says, 'you should make a vertical division of
production or invention, as you have already made a lateral
one'. The vertical division is designed to separate divine
productions from human ones, just as the lateral one
separates the production of things from the production of
images – when it comes to human productions, for instance,
the Stranger can henceforth distinguish architecture from

painting.[11] It all seems as though Plato, by making intersecting cuts, was recomposing the linear, branching diagram of the *Republic* – which divided visible from intelligible, then subdivided each into things and copies on the one hand, hypothetical and non-hypothetical statements on the other – into a table or chart:

**'May I suppose that you have this distinction of the visible and intelligible fixed in your mind?' 'I have.' 'Now take a line which has been cut into two unequal parts, and divide each of them again in the same proportion, and suppose the two main divisions to answer, one to the visible and the other to the intelligible, and then compare the subdivisions in respect of their clearness and want of clearness, and you will find that the first section in the sphere of the visible consists of images. And by images I mean, in the first place, shadows, and in the second place, reflections in water.'** (*Republic*, 509d–e)

The linear segments of the *Republic* are the outcome of a dichotomous process that leaves proportions invariant: the visible is to the intelligible as the copy is to the model, and as the hypothetical is to the non-hypothetical. The chart of the *Sophist* recasts the segments of the Republic into a net henceforth used to capture this many-headed figure: 'Let us bind him' (*Sophist*, 268c). The philosopher therefore appears to be a net fisherman, although it is just possible that he will get caught in his own mesh, given that this netting suggests the laughter which greeted Hephaestus once he had bound Ares and Aphrodite together. The *Sophist* would thus seem to end after having explored, in extension, the polysemic aspect of the word *sumplokê*: the braiding of textiles, the entanglement of wrestlers and lovers, and the linkage of letters into words and of words into propositions. In the absence of an understanding of the concepts, facts were stretched, awaiting the topology that was *yet* to come.

Because various domains of discourse are highly partitioned nowadays, this interpretation *may* seem heterodox, to say the least. But for anyone who reads the

Greek texts from the standpoint of the contemporary practice of computer-aided design, the theory of invariants by variation represents the expression of what may today have value not only as truth, but also as productivity. Inventing ever more sophisticated invariants that make it possible to account for – and also produce – ever more diverse varieties: that is the fold which Western reasoning seems to have adopted since Plato. This theory of invariants therefore has a very old core, whose 'isometric' and 'proportional' aspects were magnificently formalised by Euclid shortly after Plato. This core remains completely valid despite the connotations of such unfortunate expressions as 'non-Euclidean geometry', which erroneously suggests that spherical and hyperbolic geometries contradict Euclidean geometry. Alongside this basic core, I think I have uncovered in Plato the inklings of a general theory of invariants, but I can certainly not claim to have recovered the historical truth behind Plato, first of all because I am not a historian. Second, because 'Platonism' does not seem to need any outside help in generating swings of direction even more radical than all those inflicted on it *ex post facto*; all interpretation would therefore suppose that one has adopted all the contortions required by the corpus of texts. But above all, because what counts is finding another relationship to history that allows ancient texts to function in relation to current conditions of architectural output in order to elaborate the architectural theory we so desperately need.

Originally published in Mario Carpo and Frédérique Lemerle (eds.), *Perspective, Projections and Design: Technologies of Architectural Representation* (London: Routledge, 2007)

### NOTES

1. Detailed, constructive comments by Pierre Gros have convinced me to retain the original Greek term in the title rather than employ a translation such as 'illusion' (used by Néstor Luis-Cordero) or 'simulacrum' (used by Gilles Deleuze and Jacques Derrida).

2. Translator's note: Given the fact that none of the English translations of the *Sophist* correspond neatly to Cordero's French version, the primary translation employed here is Benjamin Jowett's 1871 text, sometimes adapted in the light of versions by Harold N Fowler and Leslie B Vaughn. Jowett's translations of the *Republic* and *Parmenides* were also consulted; available online at classics.mit.edu/index.html (accessed March 2005).

3. See Monique Canto-Sperber's French translation, *Menon* (Paris: Garnier/Flammarion, 1991).

4. Klein described them as 'sogenannte nicht-euclidische' geometries.

5. Rudolf Bkouche, *La naissance du projectif de la perspective à la géometrie projective* (Paris: CNRS, 1991).

6. One of the great failings of architectural theory has been its inability to go beyond a theory of proportions, a striking case being Le Corbusier with his Modulor.

7. EM De Robertis and Y Sasia, 'A Common Plan for Dorsoventral Patterning in Bilateria', *Nature* 380 (1996), 37–40.

8. It is worth pointing out that we still do not possess a general theory of invariants that characterises knots and links, which remains a fascinating area of mathematical research.

9. See Détienne and Vernant, *Les ruses de l'intelligence, la métis chez les grecs* (Paris: Champs Flammarion, 1974).

10. See Luc Brisson and F Walter Meyerstein, *Puissance et limites de la Raison: Le problème des valeurs* (Paris: Belles Lettres, 1995).

11. This sharp distinction was long maintained, for example, by Alberti, who argued that painting is a product of perspective whereas architecture is a product of proportion. Conceiving of the projective field through the things themselves remains an ongoing task.

# SOLIDARITY WITHOUT PROXIMITY

Platonism is not to be overturned, for Plato's philosophy does not present either a wrong side or a right side, a top or a bottom that can be turned over. That is where all its interest lies, and to equate platonic philosophy with the theory of Forms is to misrepresent a work that is far more complex than is often acknowledged. In fact, such a reduction is possible only by limiting one's reading to a few passages from the numerous dialogues. Plato wrote a huge amount over a long period, from 399 to 347 BCE – a turbulent half century during the course of which he modified his thought in response to events. In his late work, *Statesman*, the philosopher takes up the model of entwining (*sumplokê*) introduced at the end of the *Sophist* to describe the 'paradigm of paradigms'[1] that is weaving. By returning to this artisanal technique, Plato gives himself the means to articulate a certain type of space characteristic of a concrete mode of thought that is rooted more in ruse (*mêtis*) than reason (*logos*). With the exception of *Philebus*, Plato's final works appear to be defined by the coexistence – and rivalry – of these two spatio-temporal models: on the one hand the sphere that turns on itself like the potter's wheel, and on the other the thousand twists and turns by which the weaver reinforces the opposing strands of warp and weft. So we have a multiplicity of spatial models which engage directly with a way of thinking about the territory. And a multiplicity, too, in the work of Plato, with undercurrents that resurface in later works, such as Vitruvius' *De Architectura*, with its entanglement of reason (*ratio*) and ruse (*sollertia*).

 *Statesman* is an extraordinary dialogue where the knowledge of the most powerful person in the city is defined in terms of a technique – weaving – that in Greek

PROJECTILES

culture was not only artisanal, but also practised solely
by women. This technique subtends the whole text of the
*Statesman*. In the cosmological text *Timaeus*, on the other
hand, the two paradigms of weaving and pottery coexist,
both rivalling and complementing each other. The world
is presented 'in the shape of a sphere, equidistant in all
directions from the centre to the extremities', as if its Maker
were a potter working on the wheel.[2] At the same time,
the topological model of entanglement is used to represent
not only creatures and organs of inferior rank but also
the geometric intermediary that qualifies as the 'fairest
of bonds'.[3] Then, in *Critias*, Plato uses the circular model
to characterise the architecture of an anti-utopia – Atlantis
– as if such a concentric model was bound to fail. Finally,
in *Laws*, he compares the organisation of the State to a piece
of webbing, where a firm warp defines rigid laws while
a softer, more flexible weft – the preludes to Plato's laws –
provides room for manoeuvre.[4]

*The weaving of the constitution of the* Laws:

735a rigid warp ............................................. pliable weft

693d monarchy ............................................. democracy

693d Persians ................................................. Greeks

722b constraint (*bia* = force, violence) ....... persuasion (*peitho*)

722e law ......................................................... prelude, preamble

722a brevity .................................................. length

724c effort ...................................................... rest

735a legislation ............................................. delegation
(distribution of
responsibilities)

At some point in Book VII of *Laws*, however, the weft is broken. There seems to be a tear in the fabric of the constitution. For Plato is now playing a losing game: the preludes have no effect on what is woven in the shade of the women's quarters, where 'nurses trying to discover what a baby wants'[5] rush to them at the slightest sign of tears, rather than teaching them to overcome their anxiety – their 'fright', which is 'due to a poor condition of soul'.[6] In face of this debility, Plato doubts that either philosophy or constitutional reform can be of any use. Our author tries to patch up his constitution with whatever comes to hand: customs, tragedies, rumours and regulated music. But the thread continues to unravel and the cloth to fray. Plato realises that he has got tangled up in strands of thought stemming from traditional myths, where the Gods metamorphose into animals in order to seduce mortals. He makes one last attempt to take everything back to a single paradigm: the periodic movement of the stars, which eternally rotate around their own axis. This pile of pebbles, he explains, has a divine character because, being spherical, they turn on themselves in an immobile movement. Here, Plato reinstates the sole model of the potter.

But let's try to rethread the spool – to rewind to before the tear – to see what it was that caused this unravelling of the *Laws*. Before this, each of the dialogues had enunciated Plato's thinking under the cover of multiple masks. In the early dialogues it is Socrates who does most of the talking, but later on (for example in the *Sophist*) he gives way to a Stranger, and soon this Stranger starts addressing another, younger Socrates – as in the *Statesman*. This leads to some strange interpellations, like 'Socrates, do you hear what Socrates is saying?'[7] But in these final works Plato's mouthpiece is neither Socrates (young or old) nor the Stranger; instead the discourse is dominated by Socrates' interlocutors, Timaeus and Critias, who are presented as the spokesmen for another kind of knowledge, of Egyptian origin. But there are no more of these masks in the *Laws*. The main player is simply the Athenian. For the first time, the leading role is filled by someone of the same denomination as the philosopher. Plato is not the Socrates of the first dialogues, nor is he the Stranger in Athens of the *Sophist* or *Statesman*, but he can be said to be the Athenian of the *Laws*, as he is neither Cretan like Clinias nor Spartan like Megillos – the two main interlocutors of the Athenian in this text. Is the dialogue any more transparent for this? Besides Plato, were there no other Athenians who could have conducted all or part of the discourse of the *Laws*?

## CLEISTHENES THE ATHENIAN

As Yvon Garlan has shown, Plato's rejection of insular, maritime politics was relatively common, from a general military and strategic point of view, during the period he was writing.[8] Isocrates and Xenophon developed many arguments in the same vein. But there was another character whose stance would have been close to that of the *Laws*, someone who would have had all the more right to the title of Athenian by virtue of the fact that his discourse – the constitution he proclaimed – wove a network of alliances that created the very conditions for democracy in Athens. 'Some of our officers shall be elected, and others appointed by lot, those who are of the people and those who are not of the people mingling in a friendly manner in every place and city, that the state may be as far as possible of one mind', said Plato.[9] But was this not already the aim of Cleisthenes's reform of the constitution of Athens in 507 BCE? Was it not also the objective that Aristotle formulated in his own writings: 'every device must be employed to make all the people as much as possible intermingled with one another'.[10]

In their fine book on Cleisthenes, Pierre Lévêque and Pierre Vidal-Naquet have recounted how this scion of a noble Athenian family oversaw the transfer of power to the assembly of free citizens.[11] Did he do this in order to increase his own personal power and prevail over the other aristocratic families – a common strategy of the tyrants? We will never know for sure, and perhaps we should bear in mind Plato's reservations about the underlying motives for any seizure of power. Nevertheless, Cleisthenes did found a constitution that did not guarantee him personal power (indeed, he was quickly stripped of his authority). And this constitution would ensure the survival of the democratic regime for as long as Athens maintained its political independence, despite all manner of setbacks and reversals, including defeat in the Peloponnesian War and the coup d'état of the Thirty Tyrants.

Cleisthenes's reorganisation of the territory of the city was a marvel of political weaving. His first objective was to dismantle the power of the principal aristocratic families. In place of the four main 'Ionian' clans, which each had their own zone of influence in a portion of the territory, Cleisthenes proposed 10 tribes – a figure which is neither a multiple of four (the number of families), nor a fraction of 12 (the number of the most important traditional gods). Each of these 10 tribes had its founding hero, to be sure, but he was drawn by lot by the Delphic priestess from a list of 100 names, and honoured with a statue on the Agora – a kind of compromise between the demands of secularity and established religion.

More significantly, this new cadre of tribes broke up the territory and then recomposed it according to a logic of discontiguity. The whole of Athens was first subdivided into around a hundred small local units, *demes*, small communes with a measure of administrative autonomy. The *demes* were distributed among three geographical regions – town (*astu*), coast (*paralia*), or interior (*mesogeios*) – so there were around 30 *demes* in each category. Adjacent *demes* in the same region were organised in groups of three or four called *trittyes* (thirds). This gave 10 *trittyes* in each region, one for each of the 10 tribes. Hence each tribe was made up of three *trittyes*, distributed over three distinct regions, which were not contiguous,[12] and of entirely different characters – urban, coastal and agricultural. Each of the tribes was therefore exposed to the same degree to the process of arbitration that underpinned all political decision-making.

Cleisthenes thus invented a territorial organisation based on both discontiguity and solidarity. And it is this liaison between entities which remain distinct and separate from each other that seems to characterise the paradigm of weaving as applied to the land.[13] Compared to Plato's inventory of the different manual operations of the weaver, however, this territorial model seems to be based more on mending than weaving. Nor do we find, in Cleisthenes's territorial organisation, an arrangement of warp and weft of the kind suggested by the *Statesman*. But this does not mean that such mending is alien to any notion of topological order. For the objective of ensuring that the territories of each tribe are not contiguous immediately evokes the four-colour theorem, which guarantees that any map in a plane can be coloured in such a way that adjoining regions do not share the same colour. Cleisthenes, who knew nothing of this theorem (proved by Haken in 1976), in fact created two exceptions to this rule of discontiguity (two adjoining coastal/interior zones for two of the tribes) but we do not know whether this was on purpose or by accident. Plato, the weaver of the *Laws*, is undoubtedly putting himself forward as a rival to Cleisthenes, the mender of the constitution – a mender we have to salute, for his audacity in articulating exteriority and interiority in the same territory. Do we not find in this division a situation that is entirely familiar to us today? Does each country not harbour in its heartland territories that are foreign to its original citizens, whilst its own citizens form communities in foreign lands? As an example we could note that Paris is Portugal's second city, while Portugal itself absorbs a number of immigrants from other continents. The situation of interiority continues, and a clear hierarchical ordering is becoming less and less representative of our contemporary condition – at all levels of land use. In an agglomeration like Paris, for instance, we can distinguish three distinct zones: inner Paris; the western half of the city, with the suburbs and the big company headquarters; and the eastern half where the workers live. Imagine how it would mix things up if each of these zones were divided into 10

arrondissements and if, instead of local councils, we had
10 territorial collectives that were responsible for adminis-
tering three arrondissements, one from each of the three
different zones, and none of them adjacent to each other!
I'm not advocating that we apply a scheme like this to the
letter, but it seems that we can find there, in Antiquity, a
kind of audacious urban politics that should inspire us to
think differently about the contemporary city in the age of
globalisation. And, while Cleisthenes's territorial paradigms do not presuppose a specific architectural formalism,
that should not preclude us from exploring how architecture could articulate this weaving and make it visible.

Along with Cleisthenes, we stand diametrically
opposed to the recommendations of the only known (and
frequently misrepresented) Greek urban planner,
Hippodamos of Miletos. While Hippodamos probably
did plan the arrangement of the town of Piraeus, he was
hardly (contrary to popular belief) the inventor of the
geometric urban plan or the grid plan – for that had first
appeared in Greece some two centuries earlier. The
expression 'Hippodamian plan' is therefore historically
inexact. On the other hand, Hippodamos dabbled in
political philosophy, proposing an ideal constitution that
attracted vigorous criticism from Aristotle:

**His system was for a city with a population of ten
thousand, divided into three classes; for he made one class
of artisans, one of farmers, and the third the class that
fought for the state in war and was the armed class. He
divided the land into three parts, one sacred, one public
and one private: sacred land to supply the customary
offerings to the gods, common land to provide the warrior
class with food, and private land to be owned by the
farmers.**[14]

As Lévêque and Vidal-Naquet have noted, Hippodamos'
method of zoning has a radically different aim from that
of Cleisthenes, who sought to integrate the various social
classes as much as possible.

## PLATO THE ATHENIAN

The Plato of the *Statesman* and the *Laws* is much closer in spirit to Cleisthenes, though there are some significant differences between them; most notably, he proposes a division of the city into 12 tribes, rather than 10. By the fifth century BCE, the constitution of 10 tribes had become the distinguishing feature of many democratic regimes, whereas the number 12 was more readily associated with the traditional pantheon of Gods (which Plato never showed any great attachment to). Here (as elsewhere) Plato seems to be cultivating an ambiguous attitude towards democracy. In practice, he does not consider any other form of government apart from democracy, and one could even say that the point of the *Laws* is to set out the fundamental procedures for delegating power.[15] But Plato never overtly pronounces himself in favour of democracy: it is as if, by leaving a doubt hanging, he wants to force us to examine more closely the make up of this form of government – a tactic of suspension he also applies in the *Statesman,* in relation to the need for enacting laws.[16]

There are several clear indications, however, that Plato's natural milieu of expression is indeed democracy. For example, when the Athenian suggests that a tyrant can enforce change more easily and more radically, Clinias objects vehemently, insisting he has no desire to see a regime like that.[17] It seems as if Plato feels the need to constantly question democracy, in order to challenge those who think of it as arising of itself, and providing, of itself, an adequate answer to any political problem. Plato is only too aware of the fact that 'democracy' can take on many guises – that it may be diverted by demagogues into imperialist adventures with sorry endings, such as the defeat of Athens in the Peloponnesian War. The philosopher stirs up an element of doubt, so that his fellow citizens become more alert and introduce an extra layer of rigour, without which democracy is only the least bad of the bad systems.[18]

It is quite likely that Plato's intentions in weaving the fabric of the city overlapped entirely with those of

Cleisthenes, but he did not want to signal the fact too loudly. This might explain why he chose a division into 12 tribes rather than the standard democratic number of 10. Besides this, the society of Athens had evolved over the course of the fifth century BCE. The principal divisions were no longer between the four Ionian tribes, each controlling a portion of the land, but rather between rural and urban populations regardless of the tribe they belonged to. With the break up of its territorial power bases, the political influence of the aristocracy waned, but the divide grew between the small farmers who lived in the country and the major landowners who lived in town and employed a whole class of essentially urban artisans. It was this division between the centre and the periphery that Plato's weaving of territory was attempting to mend. At the end of the fifth century BCE, Pericles' strategy for the defence of Athens resulted in the sacrifice of territory in the countryside; the Spartans were allowed to invade the outlying areas while the city was reinforced against siege and the Athenian navy took the battle to the territory of Sparta and its allies. This military strategy affected each of the 10 tribes equally – which was no doubt a necessary political condition for its adoption. However, it also gave the urban population a distinct advantage over the uprooted farmers who were forced to take refuge within the city walls. Against this unravelling of the social fabric Cleisthenes's weaving was powerless. What Plato sets out to do in the *Laws*, therefore, is to fix this weaving in such a way that no segment of the population is immune from the consequences of a Periclean-style strategy. He proposes that the property of each landowner is reorganised, divided into two plots: one of these would remain in the heart of the city, while the other would be located on the edges of the territory, in the area most vulnerable to enemy attack. In case of a withdrawal into the fortified town, the landowning citizens would lose their rural residence while still holding onto a house in the city where they could take refuge.

From the Cleisthenian constitution to the *Laws*, the objective is the same: namely, to weave together the fabric

of the city in order to mend the largest tears. In the case
of the *Laws*, the perceived need for a change in the
constitution is a response to what was seen, in Athens
in the early fourth century BCE, as a major strategic error
on the part of Pericles. The constitution of the ideal city
of the *Republic* – as Plato has Socrates say at the beginning
of *Timaeus* – is to be regarded in much the same way as a
beautiful creature: 'a man should be moved with desire
to behold [it] in motion and vigorously engaged in some
such exercise as seemed suitable to [its] physique'.[19]

Since the point of the *Laws* is still to weave the city,
it seems astonishing that it has nothing to say about
Cleisthenes, the man who more than any other merits the
epithet of 'Athenian'. But this is part of a larger problem,
for Cleisthenes seems simply to disappear from the general
historical record soon after his fall from power. Plato's
silence is matched by the absence of any reference to the
founder of Athenian democracy in other accounts – with
the notable exceptions of Aristotle[20] and Isocrates.[21]
Lévêque and Vidal-Naquet have shown how the myth of
Theseus served as a kind of screen between the Athenians
and the inventor of their constitution; the heroic figure of
Theseus was also compatible with the nationalist ambitions
of the city. Cleisthenes had another mark against him –
he was a member of the Alcmaeonid family, from which
Pericles could also claim descent – which was quite
possibly why Plato did not mention his name.


## THE *PEPLOS* OF ATHENS

But this last dialogue of the *Laws* then begins to branch out
and deviate from the initial project of weaving, with the
sphere becoming the sole model and merging with the piles
of pebbles that are the stars.[22] The disappearance of other
models; the confusion of model and reality; the rationalisation of the gods, who no longer try to seduce us with
their changing animal disguises; the exclusion of every
cult apart from that of the stars in the regularity of their

circular trajectory – once more, we have to ask: how did this tear arise? How did Plato come to banish the model of weaving that had attained the rank of 'paradigm of paradigms' in the *Statesman*?

For ultimately what could be more Athenian than the *peplos* – the embroidered robe offered in a ritual procession to the statue of Athena Polias in the old temple in front of the Erechtheion. The procession took place every four years, during the Great Panathenaic festival. The frieze along the sides of the Parthenon depicts the ritual, which commemorated the birth of Erichthonios, the mythical ancestor of the Athenians, born from the semen that spilled on the earth after a failed attempt by Hephaestus to rape Athena. The festival is also the setting for the dialogue between Timaeus and Critias.

As John Scheid and Jesper Svenbro remind us, there was also an annual all-Athenian holiday celebrating Athena's triumph over the giant Asterios, whose name derives from the word *aster*, Greek for star.[23] They suggest that the battle could have formed the theme of the embroidery on the *peplos* offered to Athena. So does the end of the *Laws* – before which Plato hesitates, like a man contemplating fording a river in violent flood[24] – offer us an inversion of this myth? Did Plato the Athenian imagine a victory for Asterios, moving in eternal circles around Athena, on the multi-coloured *peplos*?

Nine months before the day of the Great Panatheniac procession, two young Athenian temple maidens, or *arrephores*, would begin the weaving for the garment. They were assisted by two older women called *ergastinai*, an expression which means 'responsible for the work' and is the female equivalent of the word *demiourgos* (artisan), the name Plato gives to the 'maker' of the world in the *Timaeus*. Before it is taken through the gates of the city, across the Agora, and up the ramp leading to the Acropolis, where it will be draped over the statue of Athena Polias, the cloth that symbolises the Athenian confederation is woven by the *arrephores* and the *ergastinai* working together in a single room, just as all the women of Athens do their weaving in the most private room of the house: the *gynaeceum* or women's quarters. The procession therefore does not merely pass the *gynaeceum*; it comes out of it, emerges from it after nine months of work, the span of a pregnancy. In this – albeit restricted – way, Athens permitted women to participate in civic life, to mix their feminine hum with the masculine hymns of the procession. Was it the nationalist character of this scene that discouraged Plato the Athenian from integrating the myth into his constitution and making it the prelude to his texts? Did the philosopher see in it the roots of the maritime imperialism that had led to the downfall of Athens? Scheid and Svenbro point out that the Panathenaic procession also featured a ship pulled by citizen-rowers, and that the *peplos* was tied to its T-shaped mast – the *histos*, a word that also denoted a loom.

## THE *GYNAECEUM*: THE TEAR IN THE TERRITORY

These possible reasons, however valid, remain external to the work of the philosopher. Context cannot explain everything, so we have to go back to the internal argument. Plato the Athenian would have had his young citizen guards and officers cover the country from top to bottom.[25] This was intended to provide a means of repelling incursions by raiders without the need to call on the hoplites, engaging all the male citizens in battle. Nor would the fighting have penetrated the city, being contained instead on the plain. Here Plato the Athenian reminds his Spartan interlocutor of the ideal model of his native city:

**As to walls, Megillos, I would agree with your Sparta in letting the walls lie sleeping in the ground, and not wake them up, and that for the following reasons. It is a fine saying of the poet, and often repeated, that walls should be made of bronze and iron rather than of earth.[26]**

But at the time when Plato was writing the *Laws*, this extra-mural model of battle had already proved unworkable, and the philosopher – who would have had ample opportunity to contemplate the fortifications of Syracuse on his first voyage to Sicily – would have had to face up to the evidence: battles irreparably affected cities. The atrocities inflicted on cities during the Peloponnesian War were to become the norm.[27] That is why, a few lines further on, Plato admits there may after all be a need for ramparts, which could be created by aligning all the houses and constructing them in such a way that they doubled as fortifications, 'so that the whole city will have the form of a single house, which will render its appearance not unpleasing, besides being far and away the best plan for ensuring safety and ease for defence'.[28]

The territory of Plato's new city of the Magnetes therefore consists of four 'sacred lines',[29] for a city has to be founded 'in imitation' of an ideal plan. As soon as they crossed the city line, raiders would be caught in a maze of banks and channels that functioned like nets – traps for the enemy, paths for the citizen.[30] But the ideal of the citizen-soldier remains, and the male population keeps itself in a state of readiness by training in hand-to-hand combat and hunting small game. When circumstances dictate a withdrawal behind the ramparts, all the citizens remain on an equal footing since they all have a residence on the outskirts which they now lose, and a residence in town where they can seek refuge. Finally, we find at the heart of this fortress–home the darkest room, the *gynaeceum*, the fourth sacred line, set apart from the movement which weaves alliances in the city.

It is here, in these dark recesses, that women sing lullabies to calm the children from the 'fright' which arises from a 'poor condition of the soul'.[31] It is in this precise place that Plato sees a tear in his constitution. It is here that he plays a losing game to the lullabies, and abandons the model of weaving only to replace it with that of the potter and the contemplation of the stars in their eternal rotation. From here on, *logos* is no longer entwined with *mêtis* and the platonic philosophy loses its enchantment for us. Plato failed to repair the tear in the half-city of the *gynaeceum* and in the text of the Constitution, so as to open new passages in a city that was whole and complete, where you could weave solidarity without proximity, where men and women could participate in the same work, each in their own way. But perhaps this was unthinkable in Antiquity,[32] where only free men qualified as citizens. Perhaps this was the blind spot against which Plato should not have had to beat when he abandoned the ideal city of communism to think up the constitution of a real city. It's for us to do better, for us to know how to unite the civic and domestic spaces of the house – and the city.

## NOTES

1. *Statesman*, 278e: 'Then if this is the case, would it be a bad thing if you and I first tried to see in another small and partial example the nature of the paradigm, with the intention of transferring afterwards the same figurative method from lesser things to the most exalted eminence of the king, and trying by means of an example to become acquainted in a scientific way with the management of states, in order that this may be waking knowledge for us, not dream knowledge?' English translations from the *Statesman* are from *Plato in Twelve Volumes*, vol 12, trans Harold N Fowler (Cambridge, MA: Harvard University Press, 1921) available at http://www.perseus.tufts.edu

2. *Timaeus*, 33b. From *Plato in Twelve Volumes*, vol 9, trans WRM Lamb (Cambridge, MA: Harvard University Press, 1925) available at http://www.perseus.tufts.edu

3. *Timaeus*, 31c. In my longer essay, 'Le Tisserand et le Potier', I explain how the model of interpolation of intermediaries in the series 2n and 3n seems to constitute the equivalent in arithmetic of a model of interlacing in geometry.

4. *Laws*, 734a–735a: 'Thus far we have stated the prelude of our laws, and here let that statement end: after the prelude must necessarily follow the tune – or rather, to be strictly accurate, a sketch of the State-organization. Now, just as in the case of a piece of webbing, or any other woven article, it is not possible to make both warp and woof of the same materials, but the stuff of the warp must be of better quality – for it is strong and is made firm by its twistings, whereas the woof is softer and shows a due degree of flexibility'. English translation from *Plato in Twelve Volumes*, vols 10 & 11, trans RG Bury (Cambridge, MA: Harvard University Press, 1967/68) available at http://www.perseus.tufts.edu

5. *Laws*, 792a.

6. Ibid, 790e.

7. *Statesman*, 258a.

8. Yvon Garlan, *Recherches de poliorcétique grecque* (Paris/Athens: École française d'Athènes, 1974), 66–75.

9. *Laws*, 759b; translation by Benjamin Jowett from http://classics.mit.edu/Plato/laws.html

10. Aristotle, *Politics*, VI, 1319b and *Athenian Constitution*, ch XXI; see also G Glotz, *Histoire grecque*, I, 1925, 474.

11. Pierre Lévêque and Pierre Vidal-Naquet, *Clisthène l'Athénien* (Paris: Deucalion, 1964).

12. Two exceptions to this have been found.

13. Yvon Garlan has noted a similar type of regulation, aimed at a weaving of the land, related to the founding of a colony on the island of Korcula: 'the first to take possession of the land and fortify the town will receive, in the fortified town, a piece of land to build on as they choose ... and in the non-fortified town, another piece, and besides, in the land, as first prize of their choice, three *plethres* of vineyard, and pieces taken from the remaining land.

14. Aristotle, *Politics*, II, 1267b. From *Aristotle in 23 Volumes*, vol 21, trans H Rackham (Cambridge, MA: Harvard University Press, 1944), available at http://www.perseus.tufts.edu

15. *Laws*, 735a, 'For of State organisation there are two divisions, of which the one is the appointment of individuals to office, the other the assignment of laws to the offices.'

16. Thus we have in the *Statesman*, 294a: 'But now it is clear that we

shall have to discuss the question of the propriety of government without laws', as the cue for a long discussion which concludes, in 301e, with Plato's definitive word: 'But, as the case now stands, since, as we claim, no king is produced in our states who is, like the ruler of the bees in their hives, by birth pre-eminently fitted from the beginning in body and mind, we are obliged, as it seems, to follow in the track of the perfect and true form of government by coming together and making written laws.'

17. *Laws*, 711a: Athenian, 'Yet surely it has been stated not once, I imagine, but many times over. But you, very likely, have never so much as set eyes on a monarchical State.' Clinias, 'No, nor have I any craving for such a sight.'

18. *Statesman*, 303a, 'therefore of all these governments when they are lawful, this is the worst, and when they are all lawless it is the best'.

19. *Timaeus*, 19b; op cit note 2.

20. Aristotle, *Athenian Constitution*.

21. Isocrates, *Areopagiticus*, 16 and *On exchange*, 232 and 306.

22. See for example, *Laws*, 821a–d. We should remember that Cleon proposed a law in 432 BCE condemning 'those who did not believe in divine things or who gave a rational account of celestial phenomena.' It was in accordance with this law that Anaxagoras was accused of impiety, well before Socrates succumbed to the same fate.

23. See the excellent book by John Scheid and Jesper Svenbro, *Le métier de Zeus, Mythe du tissage et du tissu dans le monde gréco-romain* (Paris: Editions Errance, 2003).

24. *Laws*, 892d–893a.

25. Ibid, 760c–e and 763b.

26. Ibid, 778e.

27. Victor Davis Hanson has made an inventory of at least 21 sieges during the Peloponnesian War, some of which lasted for two years (Potidea or Skione), or even three (Syracuse) or four (Plataea). As Hanson notes, the fate of the population who surrendered was invariably death or slavery. See *A War Like No Other*, (New York: Random House, 2005).

28. *Laws*, 779b.

29. Ibid, 739a.

30. Ibid, 761a.

31. *Laws*, 788a 'For in the private life of the family many trivial things are apt to be done which escape general notice – things which are the result of individual feelings of pain, pleasure or desire, and which contravene the instructions of the lawgiver; and these will produce in the citizens a multiplicity of contradictory tendencies. This is bad for the State.'

32. Anton Bammer explores some very interesting avenues regarding the position of women in Greek society. It is very likely that male domination was perpetuated even at some cost to the men. For Bammer, the separation of mothers and sons, the seclusion of sisters and wives, led to a double process where women were both idealised and denigrated by men, which explains how one was able to pass from representations of the monstrous, grimacing Gorgon and the Sphinx to humanised, more harmonious images, both set against a backdrop of cynicism. Anton Bammer, *Architektur und Gesellschaft in der Antike* (Vienna: Herman Böhlaus Nachf, 1985).

# OBAMA VERSUS IRRESPONSIBILITY: CAN MODERATION TRIUMPH OVER GREED?

Whatever the uncertainties and even the disenchantment brought about after just one year in office, Barack Hussein Obama still appears today as the only decision-maker with the authority to extract us from the catastrophes we currently face (be they economic, social, environmental, military or cultural). Regardless of whether this over-reliance is romantic or pragmatic, it does seem that our forced, umbilical connection to not only this president but also to his predecessors is a symptom of a strategic period when political decisions in the US continue to play a defining role in the world at large.

What is notable about Obama, however, is that his recent actions have neutralised the very electoral enthusiasm that brought him into office. The question this raises is whether he's astutely gambling on the long term or simply making an error of judgement in the face of fierce conservative opposition. In other words, should Obama have taken the money at once, and raced to hand it over to the poorest (an inverted model of what Nicolas Sarkozy did on his own election night, holding a lavish party for the Paris elite at Fouquet's palatial hotel on the Champs Elysées), or will it prove wiser to try and build a consensus based on social equality and what George Orwell called 'common decency'? Whatever the answer, the fact is that at the precise moment he became a global political star, Obama chose not to exercise the full power that his position and celebrity afforded. He did not, for example, form a partisan government (naming the hawkish Hillary Clinton as his Secretary of State, and Tim Geithner – former deputy to Larry Summers and Robert Rubin, two architects of Clintonian deregulation – as Secretary of the Treasury), nor did he profit from any period of grace by passing sickness-benefit laws for the millions of out-of-work Americans. Of course, those first months were certainly not without results – a desire to fight against tax havens, equal openness and firmness regarding countries like Israel and Iran, and an attempt to limit the salaries of directors whose companies have been saved from bankruptcy by the American state – however, one only has to read the regular editorials by Paul Krugman in *The New York Times* to understand the extent to which the president is making haste only very slowly.

Ultimately, and underpinning all the economic debate, the biggest obstacle facing this 44th president of the United States will be of an ideological order, for, since the fall of the Soviet system, the refusal to look reality in the face no longer defines the Left but rather the Right. It was by closing its eyes to the creation of a parallel, unregulated financial system that the American legislature led us into this situation. The risks were well known, since regulatory measures had been in place since the financial crisis of 1929 – yet they were not taken into consideration. The richest faction of the population seldom now has to confront harsh reality because their incomes are so high as to become abstract figures with no value in themselves, to the extent that all that matters is their limitless growth. In this regard, the key indicator is the salary of the directors of the US's 100 largest companies, according to figures provided by the Federal Reserve Bank of New York. During the economic period of America's strongest boom years, from the end of the Second World War up to the 1970s, these directors were paid 40 times more than the average full-time worker. By the beginning of 2000, this figure had jumped to 367 times the average salary, and as the greed of these directors never stops growing, the multiple has since been pushed beyond the 400 mark. It is important to understand the full significance of this figure – it's not just 400 times the salary of a factory packer or a cleaner, but 400 times the salary of a worker who is already well educated and in charge of certain technical operations (duties that most chief executive officers would find difficult to comprehend, let alone execute).

One example of this type of CEO would be Noël Forgeard, the former head of EADS, the European aircraft manufacturer. Forgeard pocketed colossal sums on leaving the company (a €6 million redundancy payment in addition to a €2.4 million bonus – figures allegedly generated by fairly crass insider dealing), while claiming ignorance of the fact that EADS' production of Airbus components was running two years behind schedule due to the 'difference in software' between fabrication units in Hamburg and those in Toulouse (each facility was apparently using mismatching versions of the Catia design program). What competence, what dignity can this man claim in the face of such basic failures? The case of Forgeard is just one example among many, but it's significant because it concerns a flagship of European industry and a business partially funded by public money. The more you investigate these escalating salaries (and even higher pay-offs), the more you see that CEO salaries bear no reflection to the actual contribution a director might make to the fortunes (good or bad) of their companies. And the reason for this is that the real occupation of these corporate directors is managing their own careers – that is to say, organising the network of boards of directors who grant each other these salaries. But this greed, this loss of all inhibitions about appropriating the fruits of someone else's labour, is only possible because it is accepted by the corporations and by the public at large. This strange consensus is the result of a whole collection of causes, but high up amongst them is the question of digital technology.

Let's be clear, it is not the technologies themselves that are the problem here, but a mode of production and distribution which has normalised a paradigm of behaviour: irresponsibility. When you buy a car, you can choose from a huge range of competing companies whose products, though complex, are very reliable – you expect the engine to run whether the temperature outside is – 20 or +40, even if you've changed the tyres or the battery.

With computers, the bodies in charge of fair-trading in the US and Europe have accepted that the key components – the micro-processor and above all the operating system – should be entirely controlled by worldwide monopolies who can offer no guarantee that the thing will actually work. And so the door is open to all kinds of shortcomings and deceit.

Microsoft error messages have now reached a point where they have become a kind of banal joke, the faults of this company being so notorious (even before the disastrous launch of Vista). Unlike Apple, its rival, Microsoft has not initiated any major evolution – unless you count the abuse of a dominant world position. (The most astonishing thing is that this has been achieved while operating from within the heart of IBM, who themselves came under scrutiny for abusing their monopoly during the universal implementation of MS-DOS. With the creeping integration of Microsoft, the cat has really been set among the pigeons.) Despite this it is very difficult to escape Microsoft's operating system when you buy a PC. We're too aware of the difficulty of the programmer's work to think that any computer system is totally bug free. But this inherent flaw in digital technology is amplified by the way the computer and software industry is organised – by any standard of market regulation it seems unacceptable to leave a component as fundamental as the operating system of 90 per cent of the world's computers in the hands of a single private company. Moreover, the problem is that this model of irresponsibility is spreading throughout the whole global productive and social system. How, for example, can telecoms operators continue to guarantee the reliability of their networks when the digital components all along the line are becoming increasing unreliable? This phenomenon is made all the more apparent by the dismantling of public operators, so that the user can no longer speak to anyone responsible for the service they are subscribing to. In light of the risks hanging over the management of the internet, which all experts agree is a major worry, we could well end up sorely missing the analogue infrastructures and networks that were superseded by this digitisation.

From a strictly American point of view one can
perhaps understand why Microsoft, as a national company,
has not had its monopoly dismantled. But from a European
perspective the inactivity and toothlessness of the
Commission for Free Trade and various nation-states is
totally incomprehensible. Open, free and reliable operating
systems are increasingly available to us – as demonstrated
by the municipality of Munich, which migrated all of its
computers to a Linux-based operating system. The
subservience of the Commission for Free Trade can only
be explained by the collusion of politicians and lobbying
groups who put pressure on Brussels politics. (Need we
recall that José Manuel Barroso, great friend of Tony Blair
and George Bush, fervent promoter of the war in Iraq,
had his post as president of the European Commission
renewed?) In the larger hierarchies of a business or
institutional model, no one suffers from everyday computer
faults as any problems are fixed by in-house servicing
teams: the fiction is thus upheld of a technology that
functions marvellously, almost automatically. By contrast,
the average user spends hours trying to make his computer
work, or finding some friend or relative to assist him. If
the time spent doing this was allocated a normal hourly
rate and charged back to the computer companies, the
industry's profits would simply evaporate. Worse still, to
buy these technologies, the consumer has to wade through
a morass of promotional offers that make it impossible to
compare prices or understand the costs they will bear. And
here too, the paradigm is spreading to all areas, all
countries and all types of organisation. Accordingly, we
find that public city transport companies like RATP in Paris
are now operating helplines that users can call – at a cost –
for updates on network disruptions. In short, the worse the
service, the more a customer is charged. Irresponsibility,
not to say a total financial racket, is now the key feature
of this proliferating 'business model'.

It is for the history of ideas and social behaviour to
examine in detail the origins of such a paradigm of
irresponsibility – for example, at what point did corporate

directors decide they no longer needed to engage with their employees? Some time over the last 30 years these CEOs reached a position where they neither knew nor managed the personnel of their companies. The workforce became a variable of financial adjustment instead of a factor of production. This disengagement is a direct result of the growing wealth of these directors, in line with the lowering of the highest rates of income tax. From 1945 to 1975, a chief executive in the US who earned a mere 40 times the average salary would see 90 per cent of his additional revenue gains return to the state in taxation. So the only way he could gauge his success was by the growth in his company activity, and by the creation of long-term cooperation at every level of the workforce. As a result, the economy appeared to work well for everybody in this period.

But since the 1970s many countries have lowered the top rates of income tax and money has become the sole criterion of social recognition – you are known because you are rich, you are rich because you are known. And the vector of this recognition is the media, the concentration of which stifles any possibility of pluralism and presents as acceptable the explosion of high salaries by popularising sports figures, singers, filmstars and even politicians (the principal agenda of a Sarkozy or a Berlusconi is to permanently occupy the media space so that people vote against their own interests). This celebration of a very small number of people who are fantastically wealthy illustrates a second aspect of digital technology's spread, and the collapse of all inhibitions in the behaviour of the elite. A qualified physics teacher earns a pittance, while the average starlet rakes in hundreds of thousands. It has reached the point where it's not worth becoming president of the French republic unless your salary is doubled and your media profile becomes inseparable from that of your celebrity partner, so that the people ultimately are voting for the couple.

Today, effecting a kind of intellectual debasement, those figures who occupy the highest ranks of French and Italian society are not only attacking culture and language itself as a way of constructing a world without syntax – a universe with no other rules but the private favours they dispense – but the whole economic system is now totally unbalanced. For the very rich are now so rich that if the US redistributed its wealth it would very definitely change the fate of the whole of its society. As Krugman has written, 'If the profits of productivity were shared equally across the working population, the revenue of the ordinary worker would today be about 35 per cent more than it was at the beginning of the 1970s.' (This is another aspect of the way that digital technologies have developed: the vast majority of wage earners have learned how to use computers to increase their productivity, but without reaping any benefit.) An added advantage of any redistribution of wealth would be to relaunch an economy that would be more productive, as workers would see their work increasingly valued. And the most astonishing thing in the history of capitalist ideology is that this type of reasoning was actually proposed by the American right-wing philosopher John Rawls (in his 1971 book *A Theory of Justice*) at the very moment when American society was embarking on the inegalitarian route that the whole world is now following.

Without a redistribution of wealth, however, we find ourselves in a situation where the impoverishment of a large part of the American population has meant that these people are no longer able to consume as much as advertisers and promoters had hoped. The response of financial advisors, operating outside of all regulation, has been to encourage them to borrow more, to the point where the debt of American households has now multiplied, doubling from $4,000 million to $8,000 million between 1998 and 2008 (regardless of the fact that as a nation the US survives through the credit of other countries – notably China –who keep dollars in reserve instead of buying American goods and services). This is also a consequence of the deindustrialisation of the US and of a model of development essentially based on information technology and services. To cap it all, the 'weapon of mass distraction' that is the media has convinced the American people that a war can be financed without falling back on taxes. The budget for this war, which is now migrating from Iraq to Pakistan, passing through Afghanistan, represented an expenditure of $17 million an hour during 2009, including the hours of nightfall. But in the rhetoric of the fiscal conservatives, we ignore this major cause of expenditure yet continue to be shocked by the scale of public debt. In France, in order to justify 'social restructuring', the prime minister simply declared the country bankrupt – and this was before the current crisis. The essential point of this alarmist manoeuvre was to ensure that public debt would be measured without deducting the value of its assets, as if the nation were a business drawing up its balance sheet by calculating the amount of its liabilities rather than the difference between assets and liabilities, or between income and expenses. At the same time, though, the limitless expansion of private debt has always been encouraged as 'a sign of belief in the future' as Sarkozy put it.

So what is the solution, what should these directors do with all their millions of dollars? From a strictly economic point of view, the US would do well to wait until 2013 before returning to a normal growth rate, provided, of course, that the American president takes the right measures – raising taxation for the highest earners, tightening regulation of the financial system as part of a Tobin tax, and initiating infrastructure projects piloted and financed by the state. This does not prevent Krugman from being worried on a daily basis because, as a good economist, he remembers that the New Deal was not enough to absorb the crisis of 1929. (In 1939, 10 years after the Wall Street Crash, the rate of unemployment in the US was still at 17 per cent, nearly one American in every five. At that time, Roosevelt had yet to implement a fully consistent Keynesian policy: the increase in federal spending was partly offset by a decrease in state spending.) It's terrible to say, but the thing that ultimately saved the US from its earlier economic crisis was the Second World War, which alone gave Franklin D Roosevelt the means to regulate the economy and justify raising taxation for the very rich to 79 per cent. Today the top tax rate in the US is 35 per cent.

If we want to avoid a return to the darkest hours of our recent past, it is absolutely fundamental to realise that the root of the problem is political. A small faction of highly privileged people has declared war on the rest of society. Here too, though, a little economic history can illuminate the situation. For after the Second World War even Roosevelt's right-wing successors increased taxes on the highest earners to 91 per cent to fund Cold War military expenditure. The economic expansion and well-being in the West from 1945 to 1975 can therefore be seen as a result of the way we subcontracted to the people of Russia and China the struggle that workers had to lead against a dominant class – an argument borne out by the fact that it is only since the Chinese converted to capitalism and the Berlin Wall came down that inequalities in the West have really exploded (or as Krugman has written, 'One cannot understand the world as it appeared a few years ago without considering the fundamental political fact of the 1990s: the collapse of socialism, not merely as a ruling ideology, but as an idea with the power to move men's minds'). Not that these countries necessarily created socialism, but the support that their armies could give to any social dissent in the West proved enough of a deterrent to contain the rush of capitalism. The solution, however, is not to be found in some kind of dictatorship of the proletariat or in the full nationalisation of the economy (civil bureaucracy poses as great a risk as private deregulation to the efficiency of public services). Rather, it lies in some kind of mix of individual initiative and collective regulation, the precise measure of which should probably vary according to the location and the political culture, in a fairly empirical way and at the cost of real social struggle. But this struggle, too, is as old as history. In Rome in the second century BCE, two socially inclined aristocrats – the Gracchi brothers – proposed the redistribution of patrician land among the plebeians (a piece of good faith that was not enough to prevent the city's senators taking over the land holdings in question). The outcome was that the brothers, Tiberius and Gaius (now deemed the founding fathers of both socialism and populism), were assassinated, while Cicero went on to invent the most fallacious arguments to justify his immense wealth and the Roman republic entered into a century of civil war, followed by 500 years of dictatorship.

Closer to us, Roosevelt used to say in the 1930s that a chief can only follow his troops, and that this shadowing is a condition of his political survival. Consequently, it is the responsibility of experts to explain without respite the enormity of the stakes we are confronted with. The domains of this expertise cover all aspects of society and include geopolitics, law, the military, epidemiology and even architecture. For in this field, too, it is necessary to begin any analysis with digital technology and its method of diffusion. For example, a tour of several international schools of architecture can only introduce feelings of doubt in the visitor. In these schools, digital technology has come to be associated only with the spectacular architecture of Gehry's Bilbao Guggenheim and what one could describe as a formal curvy-broken style (an imperfect translation of the magnificent Spanish word *curviquebrado*, coined by Juan Antonio Ramírez in his 1992 book, *Art and Architecture in the Epoch of Triumphant Capitalism*) – in essence, bubble forms for bubble economies. What should only be an architecture of exception is now proposed – and enthusiastically embraced by young students – as the norm. This seems to be at the cost of cultural and social factors o f urbanism and of any real interest in the digitisation of conception and fabrication in architecture.

For if the technologies of CAD-CAM can contribute to the improvement of the built environment, it will be by better integrating the process of generating architecture within the manufacturing industry. If the increasingly widespread influence of software now permits the building industry to work on series of objects that are always more varied and able to fit particular needs, then the architec-tural components are going to have to be better able to

adapt to the specificity of projects, independent of all
formal research. Here, too, it is the very particular fashion
of digital technology that explains why we are essentially
oriented towards an extravagant aesthetic, directed more
towards the emirs of the Middle East and other breeds of
millionaire than towards social programmes. All evidence
suggests that a traditional urban infrastructure equipped
with efficient public transport is better able to respond to
demographic and environmental challenges than sprawling
suburbs designed for the car and sprinkled with towers or
shopping malls masquerading as urban centres. Equally, it
can be assumed that these technologies in themselves could
be the means of solving the problems of our cities.

So how come we're so blind to the political source
of our urban condition? How can we not see that in France,
for example, the endless debate about the suburbs is not
a question of order or ethnicity, or religion or identity?
It comes down to the simple fact that we've cast out of our
society a critical mass of people and forced them to live
in deplorable economic conditions. One recent attempt
at resolving this problem was a 2001 French law which
imposed a quota of 20 per cent of social housing in
communities over a certain size. This ruling (known as
the SRU law – Solidarité et Renouvellement Urbain) was
designed to spread out those families exposed to major
social problems and integrate them into more affluent
areas. The law, though, is not enforced and a number of
councils prefer to pay a penalty rather than welcome a
small faction of low-income residents onto their streets and
into their social systems. The result is that paradoxically
our contemporary towns and cities are less integrated than
the fine bourgeois neighbourhoods they replaced. In the
smart districts like the 7th or 16th arrondissements in Paris,
the opulent nineteenth-century buildings used to include
service flats, and the children of employees would go to the
same schools as the children of their bosses. This type of
urbanism was certainly stratified, but it was still mixed.
Today in France one of the communities which most
contravenes the SRU law is none other than Neuilly-sur-

Seine, whose previous mayor, Nicolas Sarkozy, has subsequently rushed to reduce taxes on France's rich by €15,000 million a year. More recently, as president, Sarkozy has declared a policy of zero tolerance for small crimes, and yet he continues to turn a blind eye to any kind of fiscal delinquency – 101 financial enquiries were opened in France in 2006, 88 in 2007, 21 in 2008 and only six in the first five months of 2009. Double standards, impunity and irresponsibility are thus diffused through the very highest levels of the French state. As opposed to the Sarkozys, Berlusconis, Blairs and Aznars of this world, and alone among current western heads of state, Obama seems able to lead the fight against the irresponsibility of the ruling elite. And his power struggle with the conservatives can only evolve favourably if he gets backing from experts in numerous fields who can mobilise public opinion independently from the media. In order for the actions of the president to be effective, this support must remain critical, without concessions, and embed itself in the long term. Can moderation prevail over greed? Yes we can. Provided we are ready to struggle for it.

# VITRUVIUS MACHINATOR TERMINATOR

Should we be surprised that an architectural treatise such as *De Architectura* gives such prominence to mechanics? These days, when digitally controlled machines are increasingly used in the construction industry, the relation between architecture and mechanics is more than evident. But it was already quite clear in Antiquity, when the architect's role was not as well defined as it is today.

In an important article on the social status and role of architects Pierre Gros has shown how 'the Roman architect was just a cog … in the workings of complex and fluid organisations' collaborating on the production of a building production.[1] Inscriptions on monuments rarely mention the name of the architect. The involvement of any recognised professionals appears equally rare, and we have no evidence of any general contracts issued for a building as a whole. So, for example, 'the Hellenic architects of the Dydimaion, succeeding each other from year to year, were responsible only for the partial execution of an overall plan that they had no part in devising'. In the case of the Maison Carrée in Nîmes, one of the very few Roman buildings to have come down to us unaltered, Gros reminds us that we know nothing at all about the architect. But whoever he was, an analysis of the orders reveals that he would have had to organise the work of three teams for the capitals alone – a fraught task, to the extent that it is doubtful he would have had much control over the choice of *ornamenta*. In Rome, the situation would have been even worse, as the 'author' (*auctor*) of the project – the person ultimately responsible for it – was the client who commissioned it, rather than the architect.[2] An architect would quite often be forced to adopt the fall-back position of *redemptor*, meaning that 'he had to organise the funding and the technical means to complete a project, while being contracted for public works'. It is therefore hardly surprising that Vitruvius felt the need to define a science of architecture that would validate the profession in the eyes of clients. And it is not surprising, either, that in the rare cases where an architect's name is mentioned in a text, it is invariably in connection with some amazing technical achievement, bordering on the miraculous.

Accordingly, Tacitus mentions by name Severus and Celer, who created the famous octagonal room with a rotating ceiling in the Domus Aurea.[3] Pliny the Elder salutes Valerius of Ostia for his covered amphitheatre for the games of Libo[4] and, like Vitruvius, admires the ingenious mechanical devices that the Cretan architect Chersiphron used to transport the columns to the Temple of Artemis at Ephesus – 127 stone shafts in all, each 18 metres long, carried over soft terrain and unpaved country roads![5] In light of this we can well understand the importance of the lifting machines – among the earliest manifestations of civil mechanics – described in Book X of *De Architectura*. Some architectural feats, however, appeared to be more the product of divine intervention. Again, at Ephesus:

**… he met with the greatest difficulty of all in laying the lintel, which he placed over the entrance doors. It was an enormous mass of stone, and by no possibility could it be brought to lie level upon the jambs which formed its bed; in consequence of which, the architect was driven to such a state of anxiety and desperation as to contemplate suicide. Wearied and quite worn out by such thoughts as these, during the night, they say, he beheld in a dream the goddess in honour of whom the temple was being erected, who exhorted him to live on, as she herself had placed the stone in its proper position. And such, in fact, next morning, was found to be the case, the stone apparently having come to the proper level by dint of its own weight.[6]**

Thus the architect of Antiquity seems often to fill the role of an engineer, or 'machinator'. Did not Vitruvius himself

carve out a career in the construction of war machines –
the subject of the second part of Book X? Missile launchers,
in particular, helped him to construct a highly operative
theory of proportions: there are tables where each
component of the *ballista* or catapult is dimensioned as a
multiple of the base module, derived from the diameter of
the hole for the torsioned cable mechanism for launching
the projectiles.

The term *machinator* can be somewhat ambiguous,
whereas the word *machinatio*, denoting the machine, is the
perfect incarnation of the science of proportions and carries
the same range of meanings as the French word
'machination'. Louis Callebat clearly explains this point in
his introduction to Book X. The Latin *machina*, like the
Greek *mechanê*, comes from the same Indo-European root
*mahg*, which conveys a general notion of power (still
apparent in the German *macht* or the English *might*). Related
to this, the Greek word *mèchar* described an ingenious
device, with strong overtones of the machine subverting
the laws of nature. Treatises on mechanics from this time
tend to address problems such as 'How can a little pressure
on a lever lift up heavy weights?' or 'Why does a two-
wheeled cart carry loads more easily than a four-wheeled
one?' In short, they let us know that the lesser can overcome
the greater – a reversal that may have a sound scientific
explanation, but nevertheless retains a subversive character.
Mechanics runs counter to nature – that is the message of
the first chapter of Pseudo-Aristotle's *Mechanical Problems*:
'So whenever it is necessary to do something counter to
nature, it presents perplexity on account of the difficulty,
and art [*techne*] is required. We call that part of art solving
such perplexity a *mechanê*'.[7] In *De rerum natura* Lucretius
managed to devise an entire system of nature based on the
smallest force imaginable, the *clinamen*, which is in fact not
so much a force as a simple deviation, an oblique swerve in
the vertical rain of atoms, an accident which gives form to
all things. From Lucretius, Vitruvius borrows the metaphor
of the 'steersman of a merchant ship, holding the tiller …
with only one hand, [who] by the situation of the centre

moves it in a moment as the nature of the case requires, and turns the ship though ever so deeply laden.'[8]

As a consequence of the machine's subversion of the laws of nature, the *machinator* is both a mechanic and a schemer; the Greek adjective *mechanos* describes resourceful men, such as Odysseus, to whom Homer applied the epithet *polumêtis* – meaning he was an expert in the tricks that the Greeks call *mêtis*.[9] Authors like Pierre Gros have seen the equivalent of this Greek word in the Latin *sollertia* (ingenuity), which Vitruvius placed alongside *ratio proportionis* in his definition of the requisite skills of an architect. But the further we progress into Vitruvius' mechanics, the more unsteady things become: the whole magnificent edifice of mechanical proportions begins to founder and sink … into the mud. Let's look more closely at how this first treatise of European architecture ended up in such a nasty quagmire.

The first sign of wavering, at first glance innocuous, appears at the end of a chapter in Book I dedicated to the construction of ramparts: 'I do not think it necessary to expand upon the materials of which the wall should be composed, because those which are most desirable, cannot, from the situation of a place, always be procured.'[10] The architect tells us to use whatever materials are found on the spot – a common-sense principle, which became a kind of leitmotif of architectural writings,[11] sometimes taking on a bad-tempered tone in the case of authors such as Pliny the Elder, who was continually inveighing against the extra expense incurred by using heavy imported materials. But let's move on now, bearing in mind the proscription against planning ramparts in advance, against 'projecting' in general.

The second warning sign is still benign: it occurs in Book IX, when Vitruvius introduces Ctesibius as the inventor not just of the water clock but of pneumatic power too, and describes the ingenious mechanical contrivances he built in his father's barbershop in Alexandria: 'Wishing to suspend a mirror in his father's shop, in such a way that it might easily be raised and lowered by means of a

concealed cord, he used the following expedient...'[12]
Mechanics – which already has the astonishing capacity to
give the weak an advantage over the strong – is also ideally
suited to producing amazing effects from machines,
whether blasts of compressed air, or musical notes or
trumpet sounds, or spitting out eggs or stones. In Antiquity,
the machine was able to make the gods appear on the
theatre stage – *deus ex machina* – and Vitruvius was
certainly exceptional in using mechanics to explain natural
phenomena rather than to cloud mysteries further or make
them disappear in a puff of smoke.[13]

And it is this utilitarian and rational attitude that
underscores the third warning sign. We are now almost
at the end of the treatise, in Book X. After setting out the
theoretical principles of mechanics, Vitruvius surveys the
most important devices used in civil engineering, starting
with machines for lifting heavy weights – the pulley,
winch, lever, rudder, etc – followed by equipment for
moving water, among them the watermill, which the
Romans knew but didn't use, and the very sophisticated
piston pump invented by the renowned Ctesibius. He also
mentions hydraulic organs, presenting a mechanism more
evolved than the one described by Heron of Alexandria
a century later. In short, Book X, the one and only Latin
treatise on mechanics, displays, in the opinion of the
experts, 'a perfect understanding of the subject'.[14] It goes
without saying that our architect achieves the same high
standard in military technology, his particular speciality.
The subject is naturally divided into two parts: attack and
defence. The attack machines consist mainly of *ballistae*
and siege-engines: battering rams and tortoises. Here,
before evoking the art of defence, Vitruvius makes a
remark very similar to the one that first attracted our
attention:

**The information I am giving cannot be applied in an
identical manner in all places as fortifications differ
from one another, as do the fighting qualities of a people.
In reality one must provide for one kind of mechanism**

**for bold and rash people, another for the watchful or the fainthearted.**

If the information cannot be applied in a uniform way, then, it has less to with the physical singularity of the place than with the 'fighting qualities' of a people. Vitruvius' essential distinction between bold and rash on the one hand and watchful and fainthearted on the other corresponds exactly to the two principles of *andreia* and *sophrosunê* – courage and prudence – that are interwoven in the art of politics. Plato's 'royal science', or statecraft, is a form of knowledge beyond all techniques. Similarly, when it comes to defence, Vitruvius 'cannot give precepts in writing, since the machines which the enemy prepares may not be in consonance with our rules; whence oftentimes their contrivances are foiled by some ready ingenious plan, without the assistance of machines'.[15] So the machines (*machinationes*) are destroyed without machines (*sine machinis*), through ingenuity (*sollertia*) alone.

The essential principle of *De Architectura*, the whole system of proportions, is undermined here, becoming the object of a four-fold lesson in historical failure. The last part of the treatise is devoted to an account of the siege of four cities – a standard topic for historians and tacticians of the period, but one which took a very particular turn with Vitruvius.

The first siege is of Rhodes, and the events that Vitruvius relates begin with the fall of the architect, Diognetus, who had been honoured in the city until a man named Callias turned up and presented a scaled down model of a crane on a turning platform,[16] which he claimed was able to grab hold of any enemy war machine and lift it up over the walls into the city. The sight of this model amazed the people of Rhodes, who deprived Diognetus of his salary and gave it to Callias instead. But soon after, the city was attacked by Demetrios Poliorcetes ('the Besieger'), who had the celebrated Athenian architect Epimachos build an extraordinary siege tower – a *helepolis* ('taker of cities') – in front of the ramparts of Rhodes.[17] Callias was summoned to put his defensive machine into action, but was unable to do so – what had worked in the model failed to function at full scale. Vitruvius informs us that the same principles (*rationes*) do not operate at all scales. This phenomenon of scalar discontinuity, which had already preoccupied Philo, threatened the dual system of proportions and representation that Vitruvius evokes, amongst other places, in his opening definition of architecture. We should remember that the first two aspects of that component of architecture which Vitruvius terms 'arrangement' – *ichnographia* (plan) and *orthographia* (elevation) – rely on the possibility of scale representation.

Moreover, at the end of Book VI, Vitruvius affirms that the choice of materials is the prerogative of the client, while the skilful execution of the project depends on the craftsman: hence the architect's only chance of glory lies in the seductiveness of 'the proportion and symmetry which enter the design'. However he then seems immediately to contradict this claim to a unique skill, counselling his fellow architects to listen to craftsmen and laymen:

**For other men, as well as architects, can distinguish the good from the bad; but between the ignorant man and the architect there is this difference, that the first can form no judgement till he sees the thing itself; whereas the architect, having a perfect idea in his mind, can perceive the beauty, convenience and propriety of his design, before it is begun.**

Now, at the end of Book X, we understand that the role of the architect is not just to project an anticipated representation of proportional relations but also to determine the validity of this representation – that is his exceptional skill.

But let us return to Rhodes, where the inhabitants were gripped by fear. Anticipating the sack of the city and the miseries of slavery, they threw themselves at Diognetus' feet. At first, blinded by his anger, he refused to help. But eventually he yielded (softened by the entreaties of a cortege of comely virgins and youths) and devised a strategy. During the night a hole was made in the ramparts near the war machine and all manner of 'water, excrement and mud' poured through it. In the first light of day, when the terrible 'city-taker' was moved into position, it got bogged down in the quagmire before even getting close to the wall. And Demetrios the Besieger had no alternative but to leave with his fleet. 'The Rhodians, freed from war by the ingenuity of Diognetus, gave him thanks publicly.'

Thus one sees that in the – supposedly unintriguing[18] – literary genre of the architectural treatise, Vitruvius was not without talent. And the tales of three other sieges are still to be told. The siege at Chios earns only a brief mention. Threatened by enemy ships fitted out with *sambucae*,[19] the 'Chians during the night threw into the sea, at the foot of their wall, earth, sand, and stones; so that when the enemy, on the following day, endeavoured to approach it, the ships ran aground on the rubble … thus stranded, they were assailed with lighted missiles, and burned'. From there we move on to the siege of Apollonia, which once again features an architect. The besiegers had excavated mines, threatening to 'penetrate the fortress unperceived'. While the Apollonians were seized with panic, a certain Trypho of Alexandria, 'who was the architect to the city', made several excavations in the wall and suspended bronze vessels in them. Like the resonating vases or *echeia* that Vitruvius claimed would enhance the sound in theatres, these vessels picked up the vibrations of the metal tools used by the tunnellers, signalling the direction they were coming from. (A method of detection that Herodotus tells us was deployed against the Persians in 520 BCE and remained in use until the Byzantine period.[20]) Trypho 'then prepared vessels of boiling water and pitch, human dung, and heated sand, for the purpose of pouring on their heads. In the night he bored a great many holes, through which he suddenly poured the mixture, and destroyed those of the enemy that were engaged in this operation'.

Finally, there is the siege of Massilia (present-day Marseilles), where the city wall was again undermined by enemy forces (led by Julius Caesar). The inhabitants 'lowered the level of the ditch that encompassed the wall so that the apertures of all the mines were discovered'. They then filled the ditch with water from the wells and the port 'so that when the mouths of the mine opened to the city, the water rushed in with great violence, and threw down the struts, overwhelming all those within it with the quantity of water introduced, and the falling in of the mine'. But the story does not end there. The enemy plan a counterattack, constructing a wooden siege-tower next to the wall; the citizens respond by launching red hot iron bars against it from the *ballistae*, setting it on fire. A tortoise is then brought up to batter the wall; this is lassoed and 'with a capstan … the head kept raised, so that it could not be worked against the wall … With burning arrows, and with discharges from the *ballistae*, the whole machine was eventually destroyed.'

And Vitruvius concludes: 'Thus all these cities are liberated, not by machines, but by expedients which are suggested through the ready ingenuity of their architects.'[21] His point is even clearer in Latin: 'Ita eae victoriae ciuitatum *non machinis, sed contra machinarum rationem*, architectorum *sollertia* sunt liberatae.'

By reason of its coherence and the way it is articulated in the very structure of *De Architectura*, this art of defence deserves our full attention. In antiquity, as now, in our era of communication between machines, there are certain protocols for beginning and signing off a message. In relation to beginnings, we can find at least three 'threshold' devices in *De Architectura*:[22] Book I, Chapter 1, Paragraph 1, which regulates the discipline of architecture according to the principles of *proportio* and *sollertia*; the ten prefaces, which repeatedly insist on the need for scientific rigour; and the first building to be shown, the Tower of Winds, which brings together the three components of architecture: *aedificatio, gnomonica, machinatio*. The most liminal of these devices is the dedication to the reigning emperor, Augustus, which takes up the first preface. Here, Vitruvius does not limit himself to the usual formulas dictated by protocol, but recalls his loyal services in 'providing and maintaining *ballistae*, scorpions and other missile machines',[23] for which he received a pension that was renewed at the recommendation of the emperor's sister Octavia. But in reality, Vitruvius was primarily in the service of Julius Caesar and, looking again at the end of Book X, we find the suggestion that Caesar lost the siege of Massilia: 'all these cities are liberated'. So is Vitruvius concluding his treatise by evoking a defeat for Augustus' predecessor?

As already mentioned, accounts of sieges constituted a literary genre in themselves, drawing on a storehouse of tactics built up from the earliest historians. Vitruvius is, of course, inscribed within this tradition, but his 'art of defence' is also original on two levels – in the way historical events are recounted and the author's relation to those accounts, as well as in the way it brings back up to the surface an undercurrent of radical violence, usually framed in terms of mythical thought.

On the level of historical insertion, then, we can begin with the siege of Rhodes, an island that occupied a particular place in the geography of Vitruvius' intellectual world. It was where Cicero and Pompey came to study with Posidonius and Geminus – an indication that Alexandria had already lost its title as the capital of learning. Hipparchos also based his astronomical observations here, making the island the centre of his measurements of the earth. But above all, Rhodes had the unhappy distinction of being the object of a siege that represented perhaps the apogee of the art. In his siege of 304 BCE Demetrios Poliorcetes had deployed a whole panoply of the kind of war machines first introduced into the Greek world a century earlier, by Dionysius the Elder at Syracuse. Yet Demetrios – for all his supposed mastery in this field – still did not succeed in taking the city, and the siege ended with a peace treaty, marking a kind of limit to the advantage conferred by machines. However, Vitruvius' account in no

way corresponds to that of his contemporary Diodorus of
Sicily, who describes a *helepolis*, a colossal mobile siege-
tower, 'the highest that had ever been built'.[23] The base of
the tower was designed to shield the soldiers operating it,
and had casters to accommodate lateral movement. Three
of its sides were covered with metal panels to protect it
from fire, with openings at each level to launch missiles
from. However, if we believe Diodorus' account, the people
of Rhodes did not triumph over the machine by sinking it
in slime, but rather by setting it on fire. On a moonless
night, they used a battery of catapults to deluge the *helepolis*
with fire – 800 incendiary darts and 1,500 stones, according
to the tally Demetrios made the following day. This hail of
projectiles dislodged some of the metal panels and the
wood underneath caught fire. There was not enough water
on hand to extinguish the flames, so the *helepolis* had to be
withdrawn. But according to Diodorus, the siege continued
after this incident and a truce, mediated by Ptolemy, was
agreed only when both sides were weary.

Except for the few lines from Vitruvius, we know
nothing about the architects of Rhodes – nothing about
Diognetus, Callias of Aratos, or Epimachos. The latter is
mentioned in the account of the same siege of Rhodes in the
*Athenaeus Mechanicus*, but all three remain shadowy figures,
much like the 'Trypho of Alexandria' who was present at
the siege of Apollonia (Vitruvius does not specify which
Apollonia – there were several cities by that name). The
account of the siege of Chios is too lapidary to feature an
architect. But a reading of the *Athenaeus* casts a little more
light on the tale: it seems most likely that Vitruvius is
referring to a siege in 201 BCE by the forces of Philippus V,
who also initiated the siege against Apollonia in Illyria in
214 BCE.[24]

When it comes to the siege of Marseilles, no architects
are mentioned. Vitruvius relates the events in an
impersonal style – with a preference for passive turns of
phrase, like 'oppugnaretur' – in contrast to the dramatic
character of his account of the siege of Rhodes. There is also
a curious lack of historical precision: the use of the third

person plural – as in 'implueront', to represent the people of the city – remains extremely elliptical. Yet the siege of Massilia was certainly undertaken by the Roman army in 49 BCE – that is, during the years of active service of a certain military architect called Vitruvius, who received (as did the ingenious Diognetus) a pension for his loyal service to Caesar, the general conducting the assault on the Phocean city, which was then extended by the Emperor Augustus, to whom *De Architectura* was dedicated. So – belying the detachment of his account – Vitruvius himself could very well have been part of the siege.

Since the volumes of Livy's annals relating to this period are lost, we have only three accounts of the siege of Massilia apart from Vitruvius' elliptical one. The first is by its protagonist, Caesar himself, in his *Bellum civile*, while the others are by a historian, Cassius Dio, and a poet, Lucanus. There are significant differences between the accounts, but what seems clear is that the city of Massilia, like Rhodes, wanted to maintain a position of neutrality in face of a military power urging it into an alliance.[25] In the case of Rhodes, it was Antigonos, father of Demetrios, who wanted the island to join him in his battle against Ptolemy. With Massilia, Caesar expected the city to open its gates to him as he marched to Spain to fight the legions of Pompey. Given the brevity of Vitruvius' account it is hard to do much more than hypothesise, yet the expression 'these cities are liberated' strikes an odd note when we know that (unlike Rhodes) the Phocean city did not reach an accord and its defeat resulted in the last free Greek city-state in the Roman world losing its independence. The course of events was quite different from Vitruvius' portrayal.

The main thrust of Caesar's strategy was to take the tallest bastion at the rear of the city and have his troops advance from there down towards the port. Opposite this bastion was a hill where Caesar set up his own camp: the plan was to construct a viaduct that would bridge the vale between this hill and the wall and allow a siege-tower to be brought up. Besides this viaduct strategy, the Romans launched two attacks – one by sea, the other on land, in the lower parts of the fortifications, either side of the Butte des Carmes. But the inhabitants held on to their resolve – and to their powerful war machines. Caesar decided to continue his march towards Spain and left his legate, Gaius Trebonius, to oversee the construction of the viaduct. The historian Michel Clerc believes that a first viaduct was set on fire before Caesar's departure for Spain (something *Bellum civile* conveniently neglects to mention) and, since there was no more wood left, the walls flanking the causeway in the second viaduct were rebuilt in brick.[26] While struggling on land, the Romans twice inflicted defeat on the Massiliots at sea, using their usual method of boarding the ships and engaging in an infantry battle on the bridge. These two naval defeats were the root cause of the demise of the Phocean city, which continued to fight only to preserve its honour. Caesar describes at length the construction of a brick tower and a long protective gallery, which he called a *musculus*. These seem to have been the key features of the siege.[27] The brick tower proved impervious to the incendiary projectiles thrown by the Massiliots, while the *musculus*, alongside it, covered the Roman soldiers as they made their assault on the upper part of the town. This was perhaps when the Roman battering ram was lassoed by the defenders' rope – an episode described by Vitruvius and Lucanus, though Caesar does not say a word about it. As for the flooding of the mines, Vitruvius is the only one to report it. If it did take place, it could only have occurred in the lower part of the city, and certainly not in the strategically important higher ground. The Massiliots called for a truce until Caesar's return. During the ceasefire, they made a sortie out of the city and burned the timber framework of the causeway in the second viaduct. But in no time at all the Romans reconstructed it entirely in brick. Disheartened and on the point of starvation, the besieged people capitulated. Caesar had by now returned from Spain, and was soon to become dictator. He tore down the walls of the city, and took away its freedom as well as its colonies.

In other words, Caesar won! So how could Vitruvius

finish his tale with the battering ram captured by the Massiliots and suspended in the air, dangling like a hung criminal? What made him conclude on such a negative note, suggesting that the Roman army was going to lose – which Caesar most certainly did not, even if he suffered a momentary reversal? Was the point to remind the emperor Augustus, whose 'unvanquished courage annihilated all his enemies',[28] of the possibility that his illustrious predecessor might have lost? But putting aside the narrative, let's come back to the crux. This battering ram suspended in the air – was it not lassoed, then manoeuvred by a circular drive of a drum with a capstan? In other words, was there not a machine at the other end of the lasso? And was it not a defensive machine? And finally, was this machine not conceived in advance, like that of Callias, to neutralise the enemy weapons? At the very least, we can say that *De Architectura* has an ambiguous ending. A politically correct reading of this conclusion can only be achieved by changing the meaning of the expression 'liberated cities'. In Rhodes it is the inhabitants who ultimately triumph over the assailants. In Massilia, it is Caesar who is a 'liberator', bringing the last remaining Greek territory under Roman rule.

'… *non machinis, sed … architectorum sollertia*' – not by machines, but … through the ready ingenuity of their architects': Vitruvius' account is pure fiction – a distortion of actual historical events. Of the four accounts we have of the siege of Massilia, Vitruvius' is the most inconsistent. The lassoing of a battering ram may have been an actual defence tactic – as confirmed by Thucydides, for example, in his account of the siege of Plataea in 429 BCE,[29] but in Massilia this feat was of secondary importance, given the use of brick in the construction of the viaduct, the tower and the *musculus*. We do not have any precise information on Vitruvius' involvement in the siege but it seems, from reading other texts, that the legate Trebonius demonstrated real military genius, constructing a second terrace 'of a new type, such that had never been seen', and so rapidly that the besieged population lost heart. Was our military engineer perhaps a little jealous (or resentful, as the established Diognetus had been towards the parvenu Callias)? And the major technical feature of this siege is the use of brick – a material about which Vitruvius was lukewarm in Book II.

But let us pass over this inconsistency to concentrate on the general lessons that Vitruvius communicates about the art of defence. His initial rejection of the possibility of planning tactics in advance contrasts with the consistency of the means used in each of the four sieges: namely, sinking the enemy machines in the mud. While most treatises on siege techniques tended to focus on methods of attack rather than defence, Book XXXII of the treatise of Aeneas Tacticus ('the tactician'), from around 355 BCE, is full of examples of *antimêchanêmata,* from the undermining of towers to the sending of smoke bombs or swarms of bees down tunnels. Apart from the use of resonating vases to locate enemy tunnels or lassos to ensnare battering rams, Vitruvius gives little indication of this panoply of available techniques, all the better to highlight his mud-based strategy – which the most comprehensive treatises make no mention of at all.

'*Sine machinis, sed cum machinae*' – without machines, but with machination. Even in the comparatively untechnical Graeco-Roman world, it was a fantasy to pretend that one could do without machines. But the point is that, even with Vitruvius, the machine is perceived as a threat to social order and true masculine values. As Nicole Loreaux has shown, the young democracy of Athens prided itself on having a citizen army (it was seen as a barometer of moral worthiness).[30] By contrast, a fair number of Plato's diatribes against the navy arise from his opposition to the idea of maintaining a specially trained corps of rowers and sailors. 'Civis murus erat' ('the citizen was a wall') remained the military ideal throughout Antiquity, but this ideal was threatened by the duo of machine/machination in two ways, totally opposed, but thought of in tandem.

If we return to Vitruvius' accounts of the four sieges, the difference between Massilia and the other three immediately becomes obvious: there is an extra episode,

with the siege tower and lasso, following a first reversal
for the besiegers. Up to that point – Book X, Chapter 16,
Paragraph 2, to be precise – we are still in a Robinson
Crusoe world without machines, as with the three other
sieges. If we were to omit this episode, the four accounts
would form a homogeneous group corresponding perfectly
to the imagined codes of warfare in Antiquity. In Greece,
from the eighth century BCE, battles were no longer
skirmishes that formed the mere prelude to a confrontation
between singular figures whose courage or excesses would
determine the course of events. The invention of the
double-handled sword – an expensive weapon that only
landowners could afford – was one of the factors which
enabled citizens to be drawn up in battle order, one next
to the other, all indistinct, with the virtue of the warrior
henceforth defined by the maintaining of rank. The Greeks
even had a term for this, *stoicheia*, denoting soldiers in battle
formation. The funeral orations for soldiers killed on the
battlefield were now held not for individuals, but for the
members of a tribe. Battles would take place on the plain
during the day, with infantrymen fighting against
infantrymen, cavalry against cavalry, and so on. Any
throwing weapon, then, was perceived as an infringement
of this code of face-to-face contact.

Numerous texts affirm that military comportment
was assessed in relation to this norm right up to the Roman
Empire.[31] A victory achieved by artificial means such as
catapults – a kind of 'super-weapon' – was considered as
a hollow victory, since it owed nothing to the discipline of
rank and, at the same time, threatened to unleash a
technical escalation that would be dangerous for both sides.
On the other hand, to attack at night, using trickery,
seemed to be an equally dangerous regression – risking
a descent into barbarity.

The four Vitruvian accounts pit these two tendencies
– super-armament versus under-armament – against each
other. All follow the same sequence. A city is threatened by
a highly armed enemy. In desperation, the population
resorts to a cunning strategem: at night, through holes

made in the ramparts, they pour a sticky mass that drags down the enemy's war machine. Let's not shrink from the words that Vitruvius uses here: boiling water, pitch, scorching sand, mud, human excrement – this is what triumphs over the enemy's machine. Chersiphron had solved this problem of sinking when he transported the columns for his temple of Artemis at Ephesus across swampy ground. But our four accounts provide no way out for the machine: we are in complete regression.

Is Vitruvius perhaps uncovering the base of the myths of wars of annihilation, of the kind described in Pierre Ellinger's very fine study, 'Le gypse et la boue' (Gypsum and mud)?[32] Two examples from his text illustrate this unravelling of the strategies of war from both above and below. First, super-armament: the Phocidian infantrymen retreated to Mount Parnassus, outnumbered by the Thessalian cavalry. Despairing in the face of defeat, they prepared to sacrifice women and children. But their seer, Tellias, came up with a plan: they were to smear their naked bodies with gypsum and attack at night, when the moon was full, killing anyone they saw who was not covered in white. In this way they slew 4,000 Thessalian infantrymen. To dispose of the cavalry, they placed empty amphorae at the bottom of a narrow pass, and when the horses crossed it they broke their legs. As Ellinger explains, the gypsum was a kind of super-clothing destined to counteract the advantage of the super-armed, more numerous Thessalians.

Ellinger also relates the misadventures of Alpheus, who fell in love with Artemis, but

**when he understood that he would not win her hand through persuasion and prayer had the audacity to want to take her by force: he planned to do so as Artemis and her retinue of nymphs were feasting at night. But Artemis, anticipating Alpheus' intentions, smeared mud (*pêlos*) on her own face as well as the faces of her nymphs. When Alpheus got there he was unable to recognise Artemis and left without attempting the abduction.[33]**

Artemis, disarmed, frustrates the attack by smearing herself with mud. Ellinger then uses the analysis of Jean Pierre Vernant to tie together the two tales of the gypsum and the mud: 'the link is at the same time the polarity between two types of institution: marriage for woman, war for man – rape representing for the individual woman what the war of annihilation does for men at a collective level. And to establish this link between the myth of Alpheus and the Phocidian account, Pierre Ellinger draws on a whole series of intermediate texts, including one by a direct successor of Vitruvius, Pliny the Elder. The Roman encyclopaedist dedicated two chapters of his *Natural History* to the ichneumon's supposed habit of preparing to fight poisonous snakes by covering itself with several coats of dried mud – a kind of armour against bites.

In this way Pierre Ellinger shows us that the opposition between gypsum and mud continued to have currency in the Roman world after the time of Vitruvius.[34] Our architect, of course, has nothing to say about these myths.[35] On the other hand we could ask ourselves whether these four accounts might not have been the equivalent, for the Roman, of what nuclear war is for us – in other words a confrontation enacted by the smallest known physical elements. Earth, water, fire – all that's needed to complete the four fundamental elements of ancient physics from Empedocles on, is pestilential air.

**Since, therefore, all bodies consist of and spring from these elements, and in the great variety of bodies the quantity of each element entering into their composition is different, I think it right to investigate the nature of their variety, and explain how it affects the quality of each in the materials used for building, so that those about to build may avoid mistakes, and be, moreover, enabled to make a proper choice of such materials as they may want.[36]**

So at the end of Book X Vitruvius destroys the very thing that constituted the principal subject of Book II – namely, the creation of architecture through the analysis of the composition of the materials of construction based on the four elements of physics: earth, air, water, fire. In short, Book X concludes with an anti-genesis in an anti-preface rounded off with a questionable feat of arms by Caesar.

### NOTES

1. Pierre Gros, 'Statut social et rôle culturel des architects', in *Architecture et société* (proceedings of the international colloquium organised by CRNS and the French School in Rome, 1983), 425–452.

2. 'Caesar pontem fecit', as Pierre Gros reminds us.

3. Tacitus, *Annals*, 15, 42, 1–2.

4. Pliny, *Historia Naturalis*, 36, 102.

5. Ibid, 36, 95. To give an idea of the scale: Jean Soubiran has noted that the shafts of the columns of the Parthenon, made of Egyptian granite, were shorter, at 12.5 metres, but weighed 84 tonnes.

6. Ibid, 36, 97; English translation slightly adapted from the 1885 edition by John Bostock and HT Riley.

7. Pseudo-Aristotle, *Mechanica*, pr. 847a, 13; English translation by Thomas Nelson Winter at <http://digitalcommons.unl.edu/classicsfacpub/68/>

8. Vitruvius, *De Architectura*, X, 3, 5: all quotations in this text based on the 1826 translation by Joseph Gwilt at Bill Thayer's LacusCurtius website: <http://penelope.uchicago.edu/Thayer/E/Roman/Texts/Vitruvius/home.html>

9. On this fundamental notion of *mêtis*, see the very fine text by Jean-Pierre Vernant and Marcel Détienne, *Cunning Intelligence in Greek Culture and Society*, translated by Janet Lloyd (Chicago: University of Chicago Press, 1991).

10. Vitruvius, *De Architectura*, I, 5, 8.

11. As in the much later work of Adolf Loos, for example.

12. Vitruvius, *De Architectura*, IX, 8, 4.

13. Proclus' comment on Euclid's *Elements*, pr. I: 'There is as well the science called mechanics which includes partially the study on sensitive and materialistic elements. From it comes the science of making war machines, like the ones Archimedes built to defend Syracuse, and as well the science of making surprising things using breath like Ctesibius and Heron, or weight by the others.'

14. See, for example, Louis Callebat's commentary and translation, *De l'architecture*, X, XXIII (Paris: Les Belles Lettres, 1969).

15. Vitruvius, *De Architectura*, X, 16, 2.

16. Similar to the rotating ceiling of the Domus Aurea but also, as Louis Callebat has noted, to those turning platforms on roller bearings found on one of the galleys at Nemi.

17. Probably a battering ram.

18. *De Architectura*, X, preface.

19. The word designates a musical string instrument as well as a throwing machine operated by cords.

20. Louis Callebat, *De l'architecture*, X, 288.

21. *De Architectura*, X,16,12

22. *De Architectura* can be seen to inaugurate a number of different fields – as the first treatise on classical architecture, on gnomonics, on Latin mechanics. This projective, one could even

say inchoate, dimension should be borne in mind when reading it.

23. *De Architectura*, I, preface 2.

24. *Athenaeus Mechanicus*, 27, I.

25. Even a historian like Michel Clerc had trouble building up a complete picture. See *Massilia, Story of Marseilles from its origin to the end of the western Roman Empire*, Laffite Reprints, 1971

26. *Bellum civile*, II, 15, 2.

27. Ibid, II, 9.

28. *De Architectura*, I, dedication to the emperor.

29. Thucydides, *History of the Peloponnesian War*, 2.76.

30 Nicole Loreau, *L'invention d'Athènes. Histoire de l'oraison funèbre dans la 'cité classique'* (Paris-La Haye: Mouton, 1981).

31. For example: Demosthenes, *Third Philippic*, IX, 47-50: 'Now there is an ingenuous argument, which is used by those who would reassure the city, to the effect that, after all, Philip is not yet in the position once held by the Spartans, who ruled everywhere over sea and land, with the king for their ally, and nothing to withstand them; and that, none the less, Athens defended herself even against them, and was not swept away. Since that time the progress in every direction, one may say, has been great, and has made the world today very different from what it was then; but I believe that in no respect has there been greater progress or development than in the art of war. In the first place, I am told that in those days the Spartans and all our other enemies would invade us for four or five months – during, that is, the actual summer – and would damage Attica with infantry and citizen-troops, and then return home again. And so old-fashioned were the men of that day – nay rather, such true citizens – that no one ever purchased any object from another for money, but their warfare was of a legitimate and open kind. But now, as I am sure you see, most of our losses are the result of treachery, and no issue is decided by open conflict or battle; while you are told that it is not because he leads a column of heavy infantry that Philip can march wherever he chooses, but because he has attached to himself a force of light infantry, cavalry, archers, mercenaries, and similar troops. And whenever, with such advantages, he falls upon a State which is disordered within, and in their distrust of one another no one goes out in defence of its territory, he brings up his engines and besieges them.' Translation by Arthur Wallace Pickard <http://en.wikisource.org/wiki/The_Public_Orations_of_Demosthenes/Philippic_III>

    This is an idealised view of the Spartan infantry, who in reality had the leisure to dedicate themselves to training and warfare for as long as they wished, since they had slaves to work in the fields – in contrast to other Greek peoples, where the majority of soldiers were farmers.

32. 'Le gypse et la boue, I. Sur les mythes de la guerre d'anéantisse-ment', *Quaderni Urbinati de Cultura Classica*, 29, 1978, 7–35. Repd in *La Légende nationale phocidienne. Artémis...* (École française d'Athènes, Bulletin de correspondance hellénique, suppléments XXVII, 1993).

33. Pausanias, VI, 22, 8.

34. Two of the versions of the Phocidian strategy analysed by Ellinger come from Plutarch and Pausanias – that is, from Romanised authors writing after Vitruvius in the first and second century CE – while the third

is from Herodotus. The myth of
Alpheus comes also from Pausanias.

35  And yet would it be too far-fetched
to speculate that Vitruvius'
discrediting of the use of brick
as opposed to *opus quadratum*
is perhaps a kind of opposition
between mud (*pêlos*) and stone? Or,
conversely, the opposition between
stone and gypsum, as symbolised by
the ornament on certain paintings in
Pompeii decried by Vitruvius.

36.  Vitruvius, *De Architectura*, II, 2, 2.

Architecture Words 6
Projectiles
Bernard Cache

Series Editor: Brett Steele

AA Managing Editor: Thomas Weaver
AA Publications Editor: Pamela Johnston
AA Art Director: Zak Kyes
Design: Wayne Daly
Series Design: Wayne Daly, Zak Kyes
Editorial Assistant: Clare Barrett

Translations by Clare Barrett and Pamela Johnston

Set in P22 Underground Pro and Palatino

Printed in Belgium by Die Keure

ISBN 978-1-902902-88-3

For a catalogue of AA Publications visit
aaschool.ac.uk/publications
or email publications@aaschool.ac.uk

AA Publications
36 Bedford Square
London WC1B 3ES
T + 44 (0)20 7887 4021
F + 44 (0)20 7414 0783